Study Is Hard Work

Study Is Hard Work

SECOND EDITION

WILLIAM H. ARMSTRONG

Winner of the National School Bell Award for distinguished
interpretation in the field of education and author of the
Newbery Award–winning book, *Sounder*

DAVID R. GODINE
Publisher · Boston

To my grandchildren
Chris, Katy, Rebecca

&

To all my students
present and past
who make, and have made,
teaching an exciting
and glorious experience

Library of Congress Catalog Card Number: 67-10074
ISBN 1-56792-025-X
Second printing, November 1996

CONTENTS

📖

Foreword to the First Edition

On two matters college teachers, no more given to agreeing with each other than members of most professional groups, regularly express remarkable unanimity of opinion. College students, they agree, are commonly deficient in ability to express themselves well in English and, quite as commonly, deficient in effective habits of work. In some measure, the college teachers' complaints may be dismissed as the traditional dissatisfaction of the old with the performance of the young. Yet college teachers are not all by nature quick to complain; they welcome skill in expression and diligence in study eagerly enough when they find it and presumably would be glad to find it everywhere. Since they do complain, therefore, their complaints would seem to have some foundation in fact. Often teachers in the schools reply, and quite correctly, that some jobs are never done, learning to write well and to study efficiently among them. And some insist that learning to write and, even more, learning to study are always specific, never general, skills; that is, that successful writing is writing for a purpose, and successful study, study that has a particular end in view. From this postulate they argue that the college must teach writing and skills of study quite as much as the school. In short, to each its own perplexities and solutions.

Like many pedagogical arguments, especially those centering on the development of skills, this one often ends in the slough of despond. Yet in the daily round of life, we all know well enough that we do develop general skills and that we do apply them to particulars much in the way our body absorbs food and distributes it in various chemical forms to all our members. It is manifestly impossible to learn skills anew for each situation we meet; we count ourselves well-educated when we have sufficient command of our faculties to adapt them effectively to new situations as they arise. Such command implies both the development of mental habits and an orientation of the will toward exercise of the mind. It is to that development and that orientation that Mr. Armstrong's book is directed.

This little book is in many ways an unusual one. To begin with, it has a bluntness far from common in how-to books of any time or clime. Its delightfully perverse title is neither misnomer nor joke. The truth is, and always has been, that formal education (another name for accelerated learning) *is* hard. "Painful" is the word Aristotle used for it, a term Mr. Armstrong may have in mind when he writes "education without sore muscles is not worth much." However suspiciously students may look on such a statement as representing the sublimated sadism of their elders, there is solid ground for the observation. Learning something new means altering our stability of the moment. The greater the strangeness or difficulty of the new information, the greater the strain put on our present, and comfortable, state of mind. If we must hurry to assimilate the new—as indeed we must—then we suffer not only from reluctance to disturb our equanimity but from the process of ingestion as well. Studying is hard, and the less students and teachers pretend that it is not, the better.

Mr. Armstrong is not a psychologist, nor does he made any pretense of being one. He is a schoolmaster in the old and half-forgotten sense of that admirable epithet. He obviously knows students, and he obviously knows how to deal with them. His theorizing is of the kind that the young understand and, even as they resist, respect. It deals not with stimulus-response data but with the deep instinct of young people for self-realization, for commitment to an ideal. In fact, for

Mr. Armstrong studying is a moral matter first of all, a matter of governing the will—of accepting a right purpose and of concentrating one's energies toward its achievement.

Today it is a bold man who dares to say that students have a "basic obligation" to work whether or not they are what is called "interested" in the subject-matter. Mr. Armstrong says just that and, in so doing, touches the matter of learning at its vital center. Schooling makes no sense at all unless it assumes that students have a basic obligation to study; and if they recognize that obligation, there need seldom be much need to worry about interest, for interest is the fruit quite as much as it is the stimulus of study.

Archimedes is supposed to have said that, given a lever and a place to stand, he could lift the world. In one way or another, all men spend much of their energy looking for some such external leverage by which to alter or lighten their burdens; and all, like Archimedes, are bound to be disappointed. The job has to be done, in the degree that it can be done at all, from inside. That is the governing principle of Mr. Armstrong's book: begin with an honest facing of yourself, take honest measure of the work to be done, then go systematically to work.

The student who takes to heart the injunctions and advice of this book should not expect to find all doors magically opening before him. Studying *is* hard and *remains* hard; but learning to study well makes the effort pleasant, just as learning to ski well, though skiing continues to tire the muscles and strain the nerves, makes both sidestepping up a slope and schussing downhill enjoyable experiences. The students who have learned to enjoy study because they know how to do it well are prepared in the best sense of all for work in college and for life. Whatever helps them to learn how to study well is, therefore, an important contribution to their liberal education.

HAROLD C. MARTIN
former Director of General Education
Harvard University

As a busily growing animal, I am scatterbrained and entirely lacking in mental application. Having no desire at present to expend my precious energies upon the pursuit of knowledge, I shall not make the slightest attempt to assist you in your attempts to impart it. If you can capture my unwilling attention and goad me by stern measures into the requisite activity, I shall dislike you intensely, but I shall respect you. If you fail, I shall regard you with the contempt you deserve, and probably do my best, in a jolly, high-spirited way, to make your life a hell upon earth. And what could be fairer than that?

IAN HAY, *The House Master*

i

Introduction

Before the gates of excellence, the high gods have placed sweat.
— Work and Days, HESIOD

If we do only what is required of us we are slaves, the moment
we do more we are free. — CICERO

Those who seek miracles or panaceas to replace work should stop here. The basic skills of study cannot be taught. They can only be made available and demonstrated. They can be learned, and the degree to which they are learned and successfully used depends entirely upon the intellectual avidity and motivation of the learner.

How to study is one of the most important things you can learn while you are still young and your mind is still pliable. Learning how to study involves putting away the habits and ideas that have made study unpleasant and burdensome, and taking on habits and ideas that make study a really constructive and dedicated force aimed at the ultimate fulfillment of the talents which separate man from "the beasts of the field." The importance of learning how to study is not a seasonal topic that can be forgotten when you have finished school and college. Now the school lessons require study. After school you will spend the rest of your life studying legal briefs, produce-purchase charts, building plans, business contracts, medical case histories, court decisions, how to improve one's service to God and community, and many, many other things. The detailed facts of algebra, history, and the *Architectural Manual* may be forgotten. What you will have left of your education will be the ability to analyze and solve problems, whether these problems be on a draftsman's board or within the recesses of your own soul. If you have learned how to study, you stand a fair chance of escaping the world of half-truths and misapplication, and enjoying to a degree the fulfillment of your talents.

What is study? Study is, above everything else, *hard work*. It has always been hard work, and there are no indications at present which hint that science is going to accomplish a vitamin-capsule method of learning that will eliminate study. Study is the total of all the habits, determined purposes, and enforced practices that the individual uses in order to learn. People have objected to study for a long time. The story is told of an Egyptian prince who went to the library at Alexandria to learn geometry from Ptolemy, the great mathematician. The prince explained to Ptolemy that he had only a little time between hunting and military activities to devote to study so he wanted to learn geometry very quickly and very easily. Ptolemy sent him away with the statement: "There are many royal roads, but there is no royal road to learning." The statement is still true. The road to learning is study, and it is a hard, steep, rough road. It takes longer to learn fifty Latin words than it takes to dig a ditch one foot deep, one foot wide, and fifty feet long. There was a college professor in Pittsburgh who spent his summers working as a section laborer on a railroad in northern Michigan, because it was a restful business to lift railroad ties after a year's hard study. Yes, study is hard work.

In one of his many addresses to students as teacher of medicine and missionary for the improvement of teaching methods in medicine, Dr. William Osler, called by many the greatest teacher of medicine since Hippocrates, left behind him a famous speech entitled *The*

Master-Word in Medicine. The master-word in all study—medicine, music, or economics—is the same word.

> "The master-word," said Dr. Osler, "I purpose to give you in the hope, yes, the full assurance, that some of you will at least lay hold upon it to your profit. Though a little one, the master-word looms large in meaning. It is the open sesame to every portal, the great equalizer in the world, the true philosopher's stone which transmutes all the base metal of humanity into gold. The stupid person among you it will make bright, the bright person brilliant, and the brilliant student steady. With the magic word in your heart all things are possible, and without it all study is vanity and vexation. . . . Not only has it been the touchstone of progress, but it is the measure of success in everyday life. . . . And the master-word is *work,* a little one, as I have said, but fraught with momentous consequences if you but write it on the tables of your heart, and bind it upon your forehead."[1]

The time and effort put into study is awesome to look upon. There is a tendency to hide the real task by bringing out only little pieces of the whole picture at a time. We talk about only eight years of study in elementary school, then four years in secondary school, and then show the last piece of the picture as the rosy horizon of four years of college. There is an attempt to further disguise the bigness of the work of study by emphasizing vacations. There is good reason for all this. Since, however, the theme of this writing will be concerned only with the habits and practices of work that make up study, the picture as a whole will be put before you.

Approximately one-third of your life will be spent in school, either accomplishing the hard job of study, or being exposed as a slave to it, lashed always by the lack of accomplishment. Most of you have spent 10,000 hours of study time in elementary school. The school

---

[1] Harvey Cushing, *Life of Sir William Osler,* Oxford University Press, 1940, p. 617.

year is 180 days. The work time of the school day averages six hours. In eight years you have spent 8640 hours. It must be assumed that an average of at least one hour's outside study was required each day, thus 1440 hours. The total number equals 10,080. How many hours were spent in the development of habits and practices that constitute good study habits?

If you had started with a saw, hammer, square, and level 10,080 hours ago, would you not be a master builder now? You would long ago have learned how to use your tools efficiently. You would have built three complete houses in 10,080 hours. Working alone, it requires between 3000 and 4000 hours to build the average size house. Have you given any thought to using successfully the tools of study?

The amount of school workday and study time spent in secondary school comprises about 6000 hours. There are four school years of 180 days each. The school workday is six hours. A minimum of at least two hours is spent in study over and above the workday, 4320 hours are spent in school, and 1440 hours in outside study, making a total of 5760 hours—or approximately 6000 hours. How many of these hours are spent trying to understand and realize the value of the tools of study?

The regular college course of four years requires about 6000 hours of study time. The working year is about 180 days. About three hours per day are spent in class. A minimum of five hours a day is needed for outside study. Therefore, 2160 hours are spent in the classroom, and a minimum of 3600 hours of outside study. Hence, the 6000 hours. What percentage of this time is spent developing efficient study habits?

What then? When you finish college you will have used up about one-third of your life; you will have been studying about 22,000 hours. Is it over? No. You can only hope that you have had sufficient training for the studying which you, after college, commence in earnest. Beware of the commencement speaker who lauds you for the goal you have reached. You really have reached only the starting post.

From this point on your success will be measured largely by your ability to study.

The purpose of this book is to help you study more efficiently. It will aim to acquaint you with the skills and experiences that will make your study more profitable. First, the basic requirements that you must contribute will be surveyed. Secondly, the tools of the business of study will be explained with emphasis upon the value of those tools. Thirdly, the study skills will be examined, and the habits and practices for the accomplishment of these habits will be presented. This book will have no value for you now, or ever, unless you are willing to take the time to put into practice the skills and habits which will make your study a really constructive and dedicated force, aimed at the ultimate fulfillment of the talents that have been given you.

The material of this book has been reduced to the simplest possible form. Some chapters have been reduced to a minimum of rules and suggestions. This is in no degree an assurance that study will no longer be work. It is not a sinecure for the rest of your school experience. Learning through study will still be hard work. The definition of study will remain what it has always been—the determined, purposeful processes by means of which we learn. Problems in mathematics will still be hard, Latin vocabularies must still be written over and over again to be learned. If you are willing to improve your desire to learn and your study habits, you will at least come to understand what knowledge is; how difficult it is to attain, how much industry, thoroughness, precision, and persistence it demands if you are to have even a distant glimpse of it.

Learning to Listen

*It is paradoxical that listening is the easiest way to learn but
the hardest study skill to master.*

*If you love to listen you will gain knowledge, and if you incline
your ear you will become wise.* – SIRACH

INTEREST MEASUREMENT TEST

1. Do you hear the names of people who are introduced to you?
2. Are you waiting to listen when your teacher begins to speak or do you
   miss the beginning remarks?
3. Are you thinking of what you are going to say next while someone is
   speaking to you?
4. Are you addicted to the fatal belief that you can listen to two things at
   once?
5. Have you ever consciously tested yourself to see how much you can
   remember of what is said to you?

If the answer to each of these questions is an honest "No," you need
not despair. You can console yourself that you are with the great ma-

jority. You can also resolve to train yourself to listen and be successful in the training.

While listening is the easiest and quickest of all the ways to learn, learning to listen—and to use listening as one of the most effective of all the learning processes—is the hardest of all the learning processes to master. Your teachers have been able to help you learn to read and to think, but it is almost impossible for the teacher to give more than awareness-aid to the process of listening. It must be almost wholly self-taught. It was not emphasized in your early training; it is the least susceptible of all the learning processes to discipline; and it is never accomplished except by active and continued practice. Few ever achieve it, but those who do are counted among the students who learn the most, and the persons in society most desirable to know.

Now to learn to think while being taught presupposes the other difficult art of paying attention. Nothing is more rare: listening seems to be the hardest thing in the world and misunderstanding the easiest, for we tend to hear what we think we are going to hear, and too often we make it so. In a lifetime one is lucky to meet six or seven people who know how to attend: the rest, some of whom believe themselves well-bred and highly educated, have for the most part fidgety ears; their span of attention is as short as the mating of a fly. They seem afraid to lend their mind to another's thought, as if it would come back to them bruised and bent. This fear is of course fatal to sociability, and Lord Chesterfield was right when he wrote his son that the power of attention was the mark of a civilized man. The baby cannot attend, the savage and the boor will not. It is the boorishness of inattention that makes pleasant discussion turn into stupid repetitive argument, and that doubles the errors and mishaps of daily life.[1]

[1]Jacques Barzun, *Teacher in America*, Little, Brown and Company, 1945, p. 35.

Before books and printing, the primary element in acquiring knowledge was listening. A "lecture" originally meant a "reading" from some precious manuscript. The reader read slowly and stopped to explain difficult passages to his listeners. The process has changed; reading is no doubt the primary element in acquiring knowledge, but listening remains the second most important element.

Why is listening, doubtless competing with the proper use of time for first among good study methods, the most difficult of the learning processes? The practices of seeing (reading), writing, and thinking are exercised within the person. But listening takes on the complexity of the listener having to coordinate their mental powers with an outside force—the person or thing to which the listener is listening. This demands the discipline of subjecting the mind of the listener to that of the speaker.

The second problem in learning to listen arises from lack of associated control. When you learn to read, your eyes control the speed with which you read. When you write there is actual physical control in your hand. In thinking, the analysis of thought travels at exactly the speed capacity of your mind. But when you begin to train yourself to be a good listener, you are faced with a difficulty not unlike that of trying to drive a car without brakes. You can think four times as fast as the average teacher can speak.

Only by demanding of yourself the most unswerving concentration and discipline can you hold your mind on the track of the speaker. This can be accomplished if the listener uses the free time to think around the topic—"listening between the lines" as it is sometimes called. It consists of anticipating the teacher's next point, summarizing what has been said, questioning in silence the accuracy or importance of what is being taught, putting the teacher's thoughts into one's own words, and trying to discern the test or examination questions which will be formed from this material. If you can train yourself to do this you will: (1) save yourself much precious time by not having to read what has already been taught; and (2) you can give a more thoughtful and acceptable answer either in the give and take of class discussion or on a written test.

When you have learned to adjust your speed of thinking to the rate of a speaker, you have added two valuable elements to your character: (1) ability to discipline your mind to the present; and (2) you have made yourself a follower. Your mind performs in time, but it tries desperately to steer your thoughts into the pleasant, relaxing, reverie of past time; or toward the freedom of unlimited speculation and dreams which the future provides.

The classroom is the place to learn, and the classroom is the place to learn to listen. One of the most complimentary comments a teacher can make about you is, "Always attentive in class." It carries with it many connotations: good classroom manners (posture, responsiveness, determined approach, etc.), a will to accomplish the job of learning, a desire to contribute your part, and above all an awareness that the classroom is an important place for you. If you can train yourself to listen, all these things become a natural part of you.

Learning to listen is learning to follow a leader. The student who listens is the student who learns, because listening, above everything else, makes the task of acquiring knowledge easier. The wise student listens with both their ears and eyes, hearing what the teacher is saying, and, at the same time, watching closely when the teacher is writing on the board or pointing on the map. When directions are given they are written down quickly, and one is never insulting to the teacher by asking, "Should we write these down?" Again, when the teacher says: "This is important"— "It is essential that you know this"—"You will need this later," the wise student hears such words as a signal that introduces material which will be needed for further understanding of the course, for tests later, or for the examination at the end of the course.

Poor listening is worse than none. A student put it correctly when he said, "There are only two kinds of listening, (1) good listening and (2) not listening at all." The student who half-listens not only misses a lot, but distorts what is heard, mixes truth with error, and makes the mistake of learning mistakes. Gradually, the student develops the bad habit of closing one's ears and eyes until proper listening could not be accomplished even if desired. Then the student wonders why he or she works so hard and makes such little progress.

Now is the time to learn to listen. Next year and the next you will be given more and more in class that you must remember. In college more than half your knowledge is acquired through listening; in life, in the rapid tempo of the age in which we live, perhaps more than half your knowledge will be acquired by listening.

Listening takes will power; and it requires actions that will train the mind to behave itself. To that end the following suggestions are offered to help you become a good listener in class and in the lecture hall.

SUGGESTIONS FOR BETTER LISTENING IN CLASS

1. Get ready to listen as soon as the bell has rung. Usually important information is given at the beginning and at the end of class. If you practice listening attentively the first ten minutes of the period, you will develop the power to listen to the entire period.
2. Watch the teacher closely. Listen to every word he says, turn a deaf ear to all other sounds, and keep your eyes glued upon the teacher. Practice listening around the subject. Listen to other students when they speak. Hear what they say, note the good points, spot the errors, and be ready to supply information they lack.
3. Have your ear tuned for directions. Your work can be lightened greatly by following the teacher's DIRECTIONS; the teacher is working for you and is trying to help you. But if you do not listen and do ten problems rather than the tenth problem, you haven't saved much of what is most precious of all in school—time.
4. Adapt yourself to each teacher's methods. Some teachers unconsciously bury valuable information under a mass of accessory detail. Here you must overcome their difficulty; you must listen so atten-

tively that you will be able to find the important parts of information. Sometimes a clue can be found in repeated phrases, such as: "The important point," "we must remember," etc. Other teachers almost blueprint the information for you. They enumerate: One, two, three, etc., they outline or diagram on the blackboard as they talk. Never affront them by asking, "Do you want us to remember this?" You can be sure that they are making the information clear for just that reason.

5. Check every tendency toward mind-wandering. The brain, the ear, the eye must be working together if you are to hear what is being said. How many times have you asked a question in class, only to be humiliated by finding that the teacher had just finished an explanation of the same. Mind-wandering can be checked by taking notes. Writing is one of the best ways to train yourself to listen. In order to write you force yourself to listen.

6. Listen critically, thoughtfully, and understandingly. If your listening can do the same. Test each statement as you hear it. If you do not understand a point, ask for an explanation then or after the class.

SUGGESTIONS FOR BETTER LISTENING IN THE LECTURE HALL

1. Don't enter the hall and slouch in a back seat. How would you feel if you were the speaker? By that act you are insulting the speaker—the very act says for you, "I am here. I will listen half-heartedly, if at all; just try to teach me anything." Always fill the lecture room from the front; take the front seat if possible.

2. Put yourself in the speaker's place. Perhaps for every minute the speaker talks, he has spent three hours in preparation. Would you like to see such effort on your part wasted?

3. Respect is essential. Do nothing to distract the speaker. Leave your knitting at home and dispose of your chewing gum outside the door.

4. Save your questions until the end of the lecture, unless the speaker asks you to speak up if you wish a point made clear.

5. Remember that you can always learn. Never approach a classroom with the feeling that the speaker cannot teach you.

REVIEW QUESTIONS

1. According to Jacques Barzun, how many people are you likely to meet in your lifetime who know how to listen?
2. Explain why listening is the easiest and quickest way to learn.
3. Explain the two conditions which make listening the most difficult of all the learning processes to master.
4. Listening improves the whole of classroom attributes; explain.
5. State briefly the five suggestions for improving your ability to listen in the class.

2

The Desire to Learn

Time is the most limited blessing that we have on earth.

*Books help us to find meaning, if not answers, to our eternal
questions: Who am I? Where am I going?*

*The teacher's influence reaches eternity, no one ever knows
where it ends.* —HENRY ADAMS

INTEREST MEASUREMENT TEST

1. Do you believe that you really have a desire to learn, or would you, had you been left alone from birth, be totally primitive and beastlike in your thoughts and feelings?
2. Do you believe that circumstance and environment can prevent a person from learning if the desire is strong enough?
3. Do you want an education enough that you would work and pay for it yourself?
4. Why do you want an education?
5. What will your education really be when you get it?

Outside the wind swept through the giant trees that dwarfed the cabin. Inside the cabin a little figure lay on the boards of the loft. He listened. Below him voices spoke of strange things: places he had not seen; things he did not know about; the savage toll of the wilderness and the struggle those below were enduring. What was happening? Years later one of the greatest Americans we have yet produced was to write:

> I can remember going to my little bedroom after hearing the neighbors talk of an evening with my father, and spending no small part of the night walking up and down and trying to make out what was the exact meaning of their, to me, dark sayings. I could not sleep, though I often tried to, when I got on such a hunt after an idea, until I had caught it; and when I thought I had got it, I was not satisfied until I had repeated it over and over, until I had put it into language plain enough, as I thought, for any boy I knew to comprehend.[1]

Of all the incidents in Lincoln's life, this has always seemed to me the most remarkable. That a boy of his years should have felt so keenly the burden of the inexpressible, and should have spent sleepless hours in attempting to free himself from this burden, seems at first glance to remove Lincoln from the class of normal men. We think of him as peculiar, as apart from others, as not so representative as he would have been had he gone straight to bed and not bothered himself about putting into definite words the thoughts that were busy in his brain.[2]

But, explain it as we may, here was the desire for expression in clear words. Here was the desire to learn. Lincoln had it to a greater degree than most mortals. But we all have it. We are often not conscious of it. The desire to learn enabled Lincoln to say in many speeches and letters what others were beginning to feel but could not express. He became one of the great masters of English prose, al-

[1]John G. Nicolay and John M. Hay (eds.), *The Collected Writings of Abraham Lincoln,* Appleton-Century-Crofts, 1894, IV, p. 61.
[2]The author is indebted to the late Dr. C. Alphonso Smith, a great teacher, for the material in this paragraph.

though he had no one to teach him how to study and very little material with which to study. He became a leader of men because he interpreted them to themselves. He gave back as rain what he received as mist. He received his knowledge as mist, because he had so little time to learn. No one provided him with books and classes and study halls. He snatched his study periods between hours of hewing away the wilderness and fighting hunger.

A biographer of our times, reflecting upon the education of Lincoln, says:

> Mastery of language may have been that ultimate factor without which he would have failed. For the self-taught man who once would have given all he owned and gone into debt for the gift of lyric utterance had touched the summits of eloquence. Yet this, like his other achievements, had not come by mere chance. Patient self-training, informed reflection, profound study of a few great works of English literature, esteem for the rhythmic beauty that may be coaxed from language, all these had endowed him with the faculty to write well and to speak well, so that at last, when profound emotions deep within him had felt the impulse of new-born nobility of purpose, they had welled forth—and would well forth once more—in imperishable words.[3]

If you cannot find within your heart and soul the desire to learn, then you need not expect help from without. You are the only person who can awaken the desire. Without it you will gather bits of information here and there, but you will miss the greatest of all that life offers—the advantages for your life which are with you. In all that goes into the making of your life—play, work, Latin, history, economics, law, medicine, plans, dreams—you are given the purposes and endowments for the wonderful, sometimes confusing and demanding, experience which we call life.

[3]Benjamin P. Thomas, *Abraham Lincoln*, Alfred A. Knopf, Inc., 1950, p. 500.

You will never be so foolish as to pursue a fool's futile route toward the mythical treasure at the end of a rainbow, for you have been endowed with gifts far surpassing the dream-chests of gold at the base of many rainbows. These gifts are ever available to help you develop your life in every way. They also make possible the acquisition of additional gifts if they are used fully. If you ignore or neglect them you will be sorry when later in life you have need of them. If you exploit them for false purposes and questionable values you will live to regret it; and perhaps most tragically of all, the world will judge you a person of little consequence. Here, briefly, are some of the gifts which were given you, and which make you responsible—to a very great degree—for the person you are to become.

1. *The gift of individuality.* This may be surprising to you, since you have spent much time trying to "be different." This is a natural part of growth toward maturity, but you need not fear—you are different. You will develop along lines which will be distinctly your own. You will adapt standard methods of study to your own individual needs. But in your development it is wise to remember always that applying experiences that have aided others in no way impairs your own individuality. Without the application of such experience we would never have progressed beyond savagery.

2. *The gift of willpower.* Lincoln willed to learn and nothing was able to turn that willpower to accept something easier—like remaining an itinerant rail-splitter or a river stevedore. Feeling, thinking, and willing have been called the three primary functions of the mind. You may feel and think that something is worthwhile, but unless you will to make it so, it will never get beyond the dream stage.

When Louis Pasteur was nineteen he wrote in a letter: "To will is a great thing, for action and work follow will, and almost always work is accomplished by success." As a student, and during his busy and fruitful life for the whole of mankind, Pasteur kept a small placard posted above his desk. On it were inscribed the words, "Will, Work, Wait." These words directed his life. The gift of willpower is yours to be used for that most important of all accomplishments—determining your life.

3. *The gift of memory.* Memory provides you with the foundation stones from which you build your house of life. Memory, a storehouse not available to any other creatures, at least to any extent, is the source from which you draw previous experiences of the human race. It is through memory that you are able to compare before you select, and select wisely those experiences which have proved of value. In another chapter of this book there is notice given of what the human condition would become in a second were memory to be taken away. It is worth reflecting upon.

Only three of your multiple gifts have here been considered, mainly because they are so vital and basic to stimulating your desire to learn. But you have many more gifts: self-confidence, conscience, imagination, humility, time, and the privilege of putting all to work.

But what is it, you ask, that I desire to learn, and what are the skills for it, and what are the tools? The answer to your question is not so difficult as it might, at first glance, appear.

What you desire to learn is to perceive the world around you, to be able to think about it, and to communicate your ideas about it to others and to receive their ideas. These constitute the three basic reasons for all education: (1) perception, (2) thought, and (3) communication.

Perception is the means whereby you become acquainted with the world around you. You study science to perceive the world of facts. You look at the world of values through the study of religion and philosophy. You look at the world another way through the study of mathematics or history. Perceptive power is the principal dynamic of growth and achievement for the individual.

Thought is the means whereby you measure that which has been perceived. It is through thought that judgments can be made as to what is possible. Experiences and observations are weighed and evaluated, refined or amplified, and accepted or rejected. By thought the problems of existence are solved, and only by thought is the world which you have perceived given directed purpose and action beyond the native instincts of animals.

"Only the individual can think," wrote Dr. Albert Einstein, "and thereby create new values for society. . . . Without creative, independently thinking and judging personalities the upward development of society is as unthinkable as the development of the individual personality without the nourishing soil of the community."[4]

Communication is the means whereby the memory of mankind is made articulate. It is, without question, the principal factor that raised us above the beasts and gave us dominion over them. The ability to communicate touches every minute of our lives—the answer to a question, whether or not you are able to sell your product—be it a new type of toothbrush or an ideal affecting the whole of mankind. By communication you receive from others and by communication you, depending upon your ability to communicate, will give, successfully or unsuccessfully, to others.

There are three basic skills in education: (1) the skill of finding what you want, (2) the skill of fixing it in your mind, and (3) the skill of organizing it for use. The ability to use the card index to find a book in the library immediately comes to mind. But you begin to practice the skill of finding what you want when you first reached through the playpen to get a ball that had rolled outside. The skill of finding what you want will develop and increase as long as you nourish it. The skill of fixing it in your mind requires the development of good study habits, habits which will drive you to expend your whole energies in training and disciplining your mind and will to the point where success from hard work becomes your greatest pleasure. In another part of this book we will go into the methods for the development of this skill. The skill of organizing for use is the golden metamorphosis of education, for by this skill knowledge is transformed into wisdom.

[4]Albert Einstein, *The World as I See It*, Philosophical Library, 1940, p. 9. Quoted by permission of the Albert Einstein estate.

For example, from reading Ernest Hemingway's novel, *For Whom the Bell Tolls*, you learn that no man is an island unto himself, and that when one man dies a little bit of each of us dies. This is information (knowledge). It is transformed into wisdom when we apply it to our own lives, which in this case would mean ceasing to think of life in terms of our own selfish interests, but broadening our outlook to include our fellowmen. Therefore, it becomes very plain that without the development of this skill in education, the first two have little meaning.

The three basic tools of education are: (1) time, (2) books, and (3) teachers. Time is the most limited blessing that we have on earth. Time is one of the great responsibilities that life places before us. In life you will meet few people, indeed, who have learned the value of time. People fail to finish allotted tasks; they are late for appointments, meetings, and classes. These are the people who have developed little or no appreciation of their most limited blessing on earth.

School work and the activities connected with school make heavy demands upon your time. If you are not careful, you will find yourself unable to do the things you are particularly eager to do. School life is planned this way in order to force you to budget your time and become a master of yourself, so that you may reap the full reward of this most responsible discipline. "So teach us to number our days, that we may apply our hearts unto wisdom" (Psalms 90:12).

In school work, as in sports, business ventures, and military campaigns, it is essential to have a plan of action. The student who develops system and regularity in study habits, budgets one's time properly, and then adheres to the system and schedule has doubled the effectiveness of work and eliminated the worry and anxious anticipation from this, the most formative and important part of life. A schedule that is steadily followed soon becomes the easy and natural routine of the day. Constant repetition makes a good habit a part of the person who practices it. By following carefully the study schedule which you prepare, you can acquire that most precious of all knowledge—the power to work. You must build your schedule for work (and play) upon tangible and intangible factors: What are your capabilities? What are your limitations? What are your strengths? What are your desires? What are your aims? Only you can determine the value of system and schedule, only you can build within yourself an appreciation of the value of time, only you can determine a proper method of attack, only you can achieve system and regularity, and only you can realize the reward from time properly allotted.

The second basic tool in education is books. In another part of this book a whole chapter is devoted to this important tool. A brief acquaintance here, however, seems necessary. Books are the memory of mankind. They are one of the several important things without which our race would not be what we call "human," as distinguished from what we call "animal." This tool of education, this memory of mankind, this great legacy, this lever that lifted us out of savagery, this enables us to find ourselves. Here the aims of education and its purposes for us are made clear by the hopes, aspirations, conflicts, experiences, successes, and failures of people in time and space who are one with us. In books we become a part of the great drama which we call life. Without books education would possess no articulate spirit, and our function would be survival rather than aspiration.

The third tool in education is teachers. In a broad sense we are all teachers; by example we are teaching those around us. Here we are concerned with the teachers who serve as your partners in the greatest endeavor and undertaking of your life—your education. How must you use this tool? You can be shown "the high, white star of Truth," and bidden to "gaze and there aspire." You must be keenly aware that a partnership exists between you and your teacher. So often, students speak of doing an assignment, writing a paper, preparing a test, for _____, the teacher. You are not doing these things for _____; you are doing them for yourself. The great enterprise is yours; the teacher is a minor partner in the enterprise. The teacher can open windows of vision and point to horizons beyond, but the horizons belong to you. The teacher can be "as the shadow of a mighty rock in a weary land," but only you can find shelter from sun, wind, and sand in the shadow of the mighty rock. The teacher is the guidepost for the journey, but the journey is yours. The teacher can light the lantern and put it in your hand, but you must walk into the dark.

REVIEW QUESTIONS

1. What are some of your natural gifts always ready to stimulate your desire to learn?
2. What are the three basic reasons for education?
3. Explain briefly what is meant by each of the basic reasons for education.
4. What are the three basic skills in education? Explain the third.
5. What are the three basic tools of education? Which is the most limited?

Using the Tools

The present is the only thing of which a man can be deprived.
— MARCUS AURELIUS, *Meditations*

The most valuable result of all education is to make you do the thing you have to do, when it ought to be done, whether you like it or not. —THOMAS HUXLEY

INTEREST MEASUREMENT TEST

1. Have you ever followed a daily schedule for work and play which you, yourself, made?
2. Do you frequently turn in assignments late?
3. Do you consider yourself thoughtless and rude when you are late to appointments?
4. Do you, without looking, know the name of the author of any of your textbooks?
5. Do you believe that, other than your parents, the people who will most influence your life for good are your teachers?

The secret of how to study is locked up in the desire to learn. Good students are not "born students"; good students are made by constant and deliberate practice of good study habits, and for this there is absolutely no substitute. The first of these habits is the proper use of time. Even though you feel that you cannot be the best student in your class, you will be surprised at the sudden improvement that will develop out of a sensible routine. Do not be frightened by the term "sensible routine"; it merely means order. Order presupposes that all-important quality which must come from within yourself—the desire to be a good student. This responsibility is yours. Your parents cannot wish it upon you, and your teachers cannot force it upon you. You must first *want* to be a good student.

"How can you take the greatest possible advantage of your capacities with the least possible strain?" asked Dr. William Osler of his beginning medical students. Then he would answer the question for them:

> By cultivating system. I say cultivating advisedly, since some of you will find the acquisition of systematic habits very hard. There are minds congenitally [born] systematic; others have a lifelong fight against an inherited tendency to diffuseness and carelessness in work. Take away with you, from a man who has had to fight a hard battle, the profound conviction of the value of system in your work. To follow the routine of the classes is easy enough, but to take routine into every part of your daily life is hard work. Let each hour of the day have its allotted duty, and cultivate that power of concentration which grows with its exercise, so that the attention neither flags nor wavers, but settles with a bull-dog tenacity on the subject before you. Constant repetition makes a good habit fit easily in your mind, and by the end of the session you may have gained that most precious of all knowledge—the power to work.[1]

In order to form good study habits you must know what you are going to study and when you are going to study. Both of these impor-

[1]Harvey Cushing, *The life of Sir William Osler*, Oxford University Press, 1940, p. 619.

tant aids to study can be accomplished by a very simple device, a satisfactory plan book. One that might be recommended is the *Student Daily Planner.** It is a compact little book, arranged so that your whole week's work schedule and assignments are spread out before you.

The diagram does not give a complete picture. The space for each period is large enough so that you can also write in detailed assignments.

Monday, Sept. 10	Tuesday, Sept. 11
Latin II	English II X
pages 4–6	Grammar Usage—pages 4–8
Study carefully all information on pages 4–5.	Write Ex. II on page 6.
Translate Ex. I on page 5.	Theme due Saturday. Miltiades at Marathon.

A carefully worked out study schedule is essential to good study habits. In the study schedule shown, the student starts the week with all work prepared. He or she will be far ahead during the entire week with a period designated for the study of each subject. An orderly program saves time so that there will be time to enjoy some of the things that might otherwise be missed. If you know that you are going to study Latin the third period, or from 7:30 to 8:30 P.M., the time that might be wasted looking at one book and then another, moving from one chair to another, shifting from dream to reality, will be saved. Without an efficient schedule more time is spent getting ready to study than is spent at actual study.

Many people wonder constantly where their time goes, but few ever bother to analyze a day and find out. In order to convince yourself that a study schedule, carefully followed, would save you much time and give you many study advantages, you should keep a time chart of

Student Daily Planner published by Elan Pub. Co. Inc., P. O. Box 683, Meredith, NH 03253

Study Schedule

Subject and Period	Monday	Tuesday	Wednesday	Thursday	Friday	Saturday
1	Latin II	Review Conf. Period[b]	Latin II	Latin II	Latin II	
2	Study Latin for Wed.[a]	Study History for Wed.	Review Conf. Period[b]	Study Latin for Fri.	Study Latin for Mon.	
3	Math. II	Math. II	Math. II	Conf. Period Math. II	Study Math. for Mon.	
4	English II	English II	Study Math. for Thurs.	English II	Conf. Period Review	English II
5	History II	Study Math. for Wed.	History II	History II	History II	
6	Study Math. for Tues.	Study English for Thurs.	Study History for Fri.	Study History for Mon.	Study History for Mon.	Over week end study all subjects
Afternoon Activities						
Evening	Study English for Tues.	Study English Read Write themes	Study Latin for Thurs.	Study English for Sat.	Review	

[a] If the habit of studying assignments well in advance is formed, you will never again practice the old habit of "getting under the wire."
[b] The term "Conference Period" designates a period for consultation with your teachers. Some schools practice this as a definite part of the day's schedule.

Time Use Chart: Monday, September 5

A.M.

8–9   Arrived at school 8:30

Talked with friends 8:30–9

9–10   Chemistry class

10–11   Study period. Went to school library—read magazine.

11–12   History class

P.M.

12–1   Lunch for half hour.

Cannot remember what I did until 1 P.M.

1–2   English class

2–3   Math. class

3–4   3–3:30 travel home

3:30–4 snack, telephone, etc.

4–5   Met friend at drugstore.

5–6   Read English assignment 15 min. Listened to records.

6–7   Dinner

7–8

8–9

9–10

Total hours (excepting two hours for meals)	12
Time in class	4
Time studying outside of class	____
Time in social activity and recreation	
(talking, drugstore, telephone, records, etc.)	____
Time otherwise accounted for	____
Time not accounted for	____

your waking hours for a week or two. Only by being honest and doing a sincere job of self-discovery and evaluation can you improve. Your time chart can be drawn very simply after the model on page 00.

The schedule should be made out before the week starts. It should be followed daily, weekly, monthly, until it becomes a natural part of your program. It cannot be done the first week and then forgotten—not if you expect any help from it. It will only be helpful in direct proportion to the thought and effort you put into it.

Do not expect a week's trial to establish the habit. You will want to change your schedule from time to time as emphasis on one subject or another demands more or less time. One thing is certain; a schedule will never become a real study aid unless you make it so. It can be a great aid; as Ralph Waldo Emerson wrote, "Nothing great was ever accomplished without enthusiasm." Therefore, be enthusiastic enough to work out two or three study models. Here a second model is offered. It is slightly different from the preceding one. You can probably make one much more efficient for your own needs.

Avoid being too heroic in establishing your study schedule. Your capacities vary. You will need more time for one subject than for another; this you must determine as quickly as possible and adjust accordingly. Your schedule should be rigid enough to be effective, yet flexible enough to take care of ever recurring emergencies. A well-organized schedule will not only bring order to the time element of your existence but will affect an orderly approach to all elements of your life.

Research by psychologists and efficiency experts has resulted in impressive statistics that relate the advantages of well-organized time and time-product factors. "If we have," writes Dr. B. C. Ewer, "several duties confronting us, simultaneously, it is only too likely that we shall fail to do any of them. They seem to get in each other's way. The pressure of each prevents us from giving ourselves whole-heartedly to any, or we turn in futile fashion from one to another, dropping each as soon as it is begun."[2]

Time Schedule

Twelve Precious Hours	Monday	Tuesday	Wednesday	Thursday	Friday	Saturday	Sunday
8–9	8–8:30 Bus to school; review one subject						
9–10	Chemistry class						
10–11	English class						
11–12	Study Chem. for Tues.	Study Chem. for Wed.	Study Chem. for Thurs.	Study for Chem. Test Fri.	Study Chem. for Mon.	Study English for Mon.	
1–2	Math. class					Good study time	
2–3	History class						
3–4	Home and exercise						

Time					
4–5	Recreation			Study for Chem. test	
5–6	Study Math. for Tues.	Study Math. for Wed.	Study Math. for Thurs.	Study Math. for Fri.	Study Math. for Mon.
7–8	Study Hist. for Tues.	Study Hist. for Wed.	Study Hist. for Thurs.	Study Hist. for Fri.	Study Hist. for Mon.
8–9	Study Eng. for Tues.	Study Eng. for Wed.	Study Eng. for Thurs.	Study Eng. for Fri.	Recreation
9–10	Relax and read	Listen to music			
	Comments	Comments	Comments	Comments	Comments	Comments
	All work finished.				A good week. Grades up.	

Does Dr. Ewer's comment not recall the way you have dealt with three or four assignments?

The people whom you encounter in reading biographies, the people who have made the world better, the people who have achieved success, are the people who have learned to make time serve them. Invariably their work habits show a well-designed pattern or schedule. In reality such a schedule becomes one of your great responsibilities in life. The person who fails in this responsibility becomes a hanger-on, a liability; and most tragic of all, they sometimes becomes an unbearable burden to themselves.

HOW TO USE THE BOOKS

You have already noted in Chapter Two that books are the memory of mankind. Books constitute your second most important tool in education. In school your chief concern is with textbooks. What is a textbook? A textbook presents the principles of a subject; it is the basis of instruction. It is the foundation upon which you build; it is the springboard from which you dive into the world of thought and learning. The function of the textbook is to provide a "beginning."

You are reluctant to enter upon a venture unless you have first surveyed it. So it should be with each assignment in your textbook. You should first survey the book. See what you are going to study; even a brief survey of the table of contents is better than nothing. As you begin an assignment make a *preliminary survey* of the assignment. The preliminary survey will vary in different courses and different books and can be modified to your own peculiar needs. These variants will be taken up in the chapters dealing with specific subjects, but the general form for the reading assignment makes a good beginning.

Variations will become evident as you begin to organize your work, but the preliminary survey will consist mainly of the following:

[2]B. C. Ewer, *Applied Psychology,* The Macmillan Company, 1945, p. 238.

(1) Study the chapter title; relate the topic to what you have studied before. (2) Study the section headings if the book is so constructed; this gives you the broad divisions of the topic. (3) Study the paragraph headings; this puts you on speaking terms with the subject matter of the chapter or assignment. Having made the preliminary survey you know what you are going to learn from the assignment, and you already know, in five minutes, more than the person who has started with the first sentence and waded laboriously through the whole assignment, with no achievement other than being able to say to the teacher, "Yes, I read every word." The few minutes spent on the preliminary survey will save you much time because it will afford you a background for understanding *what you are reading* and *why you are reading it*. Neglect this preliminary survey and you become lost in details, unable to see how they are related to each other, unable to establish a relationship between what you have studied and what you are studying.

The textbook is arranged as a guide to help you from one important point of interest to the next. It is actually a series of mental stepping stones leading to one of two heights—information and knowledge. The rules, the definitions, the notes all have bearing upon the next step. Ignore them and you cannot hope to write the exercise, solve the problem, or convert the information into knowledge. The student who ignores rules and definitions is all too soon overcome by ideas that cannot be understood. Without mastery of the fundamentals, you work toward disaster.

The student who accomplishes the difficult task of effective study is not satisfied with a preliminary survey, followed by a thorough study of the assignment. The real student goes one step farther, making a final survey to be sure of what has been studied. The one outstandingly inefficient method of study used by the failing student is to read an assignment over and over, ad infinitum then close the book without the slightest idea of what has been absorbed and not absorbed about the assignment. Unless you check by asking yourself what you have studied, you can neither locate nor remedy your weak points. Reciting to yourself is one of the best ways of clinching the essential information of an assignment, and it is the first step in converting information into knowledge.

Since your book is a tool and your own possession, use it as such. Read footnotes and information under illustrations. Make use of questions, study helps, and review exercises at the end of the chapter if the book provides such. Learn the time-saving purpose of the index. The textbook is a tool only if used wisely; it is a burden and obstacle if approached blindly and without interest.

Probably the greatest single source of information available to the majority of students is the textbook. The most practiced classroom activity is some type of elaboration of textbook material. It is the common ground where student and teacher meet. It is doubtless true that more student hours are spent in studying textbooks than in any other form of study. While the nature of textbooks in different subjects varies greatly, the fundamental practices for successful study are basically the same for all books.

The following suggestions have proved successful in giving students more respect for the material they are required to study, and more self-confidence in their approach and mastery of the material in the textbook. Try them on your own assignments.

RULES FOR BETTER TEXTBOOK USE

1. Own your book, have your name written in it (unless it is state property), and always take it to class with you.
2. Know the author, and something about him or her if possible. Study the plan of the book, the organization of material, and the nature and purpose of all illustrative material.
3. The textbook does not have an obligation except to present the material. You have a basic obligation for accepting the book and developing interest in what it offers.
4. There is a best procedure for doing everything, and so it is with the

study of a textbook. Find the best procedure, adapt it to your specific needs, and use it.

5. Think of your textbook, not as so many pages, but as cumulative knowledge, arranged in logical topical steps designed to aid you in moving forward and upward, and use it to that end rather than to study a ten-page assignment day after day for no more reason than to get a passing mark. Study to learn and the mark will take care of itself.

YOU AND YOUR TEACHERS

Aside from your parents, the people who will exert the most lasting influence upon your life will be your teachers. Teaching and learning are inseparable. You and your teachers will learn together. Your teachers will learn from you exactly what your hopes and aspirations are, and to what extent you will expend yourself to realize them. You will learn from your teachers that they are selfless in their efforts to be minor partners in the greatest enterprise of your life.

You will demand much of your teachers, but what you get is your responsibility. It is not the function of the teacher to thrust something upon you which you do not want. A teacher has nothing to do with creating either the mind or the heart of the student, but can only help to develop them. A good teacher hopes and tries to make you conscious of the potentialities that are within you.

Look, listen, and *learn* may be called the three basic precepts for effective use of your teachers. Teachers are impressed by your classroom manners. There are good classroom manners just as there are good afternoon tea manners. The way you enter a classroom, your posture and expression while in class, the way you leave a classroom— all these little actions and impressions reveal much to your teachers.

Classroom efficiency results from attentiveness and willingness to learn. You will soon note that the good students maintain a high standard of classroom efficiency. They are aware of the value of the many hours spent in the classroom and they use these hours to the best possible advantage. Some students spend much study time learning material that could have been learned during class time, save for lack of attentiveness.

Two simple tests can give you a sound estimate of what your role in the classroom is. First, make an estimate of what the class would be like if all the people in it acted and responded as you do. Would there be a general air of indifference and inattention, or would there prevail a sense of responsibility and willingness to learn? Would the class time be taken up with stupid questions and excuses for not being able to reply, or would intelligent discussion and well-organized response contribute much to all?

Now examine the strength or weakness of this important joint venture by the second test: Put yourself in the teacher's place. Is your work the quality that you would like if you were the teacher? Do you respond to correction and help as you yourself would like? If you were the teacher would you pick you as one of the most diligent and cooperative members of the class? You may not be the smartest person in the class, but you can be the most responsive and appreciative.

Every teacher knows that he or she is not teaching to all the people in any given class. Some are there for the social ride, some because their parents require it, some because the state is willing to spend money to buy something precious for somebody who won't accept it, and some are there because they want to learn. If you were the teacher, in which of these groups would you place yourself? And if you were the teacher, one of the most complimentary things you could ever say about one of your students would be, "This student wants to learn." What do your teachers say of you?

In a poem entitled *In a Classroom* the poet, John Holmes, speaks for the teacher:

I am asking you what you want to be,
Asking you what you want of me.
Telling you there is nothing in yourself
Ever to fear.
And wondering if you hear.[3]

Your teacher is working for you. Listen carefully to what is said, note the items that are considered to be most important, observe carefully as the "hard spots" and the "high spots" are explained. Listen to distinguish between essentials and nonessentials. Always remember that what is done in the classroom has a primary purpose—to help you learn. The least you can do is listen attentively and eagerly; not to do this is to brand yourself a waster-of-opportunity in the eyes of your teacher.

Remember, you are working for yourself. You have doubtless heard, "I have a theme to write for _____. I have thirty pages to read for _____. I have ten sentences to write for old _____." Nothing could be further from the truth. You do a lot of work in school, but none of it is done for the teacher. You are working to develop not the teacher but yourself. Realize this once and for all and you will come to know that a person does a better job when in business for himself or herself.

REVIEW QUESTIONS

1. Relate in a well-organized paragraph Dr. William Osler's advice to his students concerning the value of system in work.
2. List as many benefits as you can that result from a good, well-followed study schedule.
3. Is Dr. B. C. Ewer's comment on the psychology of procrastination true to human nature? Explain.
4. Relate the five suggestions for better textbook use.
5. What are some of the benefits which result from classroom efficiency?

---

[3]John Holmes, *Map of My Country*, Duell, Sloan & Pearce. Copyright, 1943 by John Holmes.

Getting More From What You Read

*If you do not read good books you have no advantage over the
person who cannot read them.* —MARK TWAIN

*There is no such thing as an interesting book, there are only
interested readers.* —EMERSON

INTEREST MEASUREMENT TEST

1. When you have read a book do you feel that you have talked with, and come to know, the author?
2. Do you read for pleasure, choosing to read when there are other things to do, or do you read only to escape your own boredom?
3. When you begin to read a book or assignment do you honestly expect to remember most of what you read?
4. Do you use each reading experience as a practice period in improving comprehension and increasing speed, or do you read today's assignments exactly the way you read yesterday's—assuming that you know how to read and that is the end of it?
5. Do you really believe that you can improve your reading? Do you think a runner would ever win a race if, at the start, he or she did not believe themselves capable of winning?

"The dear good people don't know how long it takes to learn to read. I've been at it eighty years, and can't say yet that I've reached the goal." These are words from the great genius Wolfgang von Goethe, whose writings comprise a hundred and fifteen volumes.

WHAT READING IS NOT

There are several injurious things that are not reading but are practiced as such—at great loss to the reader. First of all, reading does not consist of looking at each individual word on the page. Indeed, few pages are worthy of such attention, and you are not morally obligated (as many students think) to paw over each word. Secondly, reading does not consist of slow, laborious memorization of the printed page, although a good reader retains a surprising amount of what he reads—if he wills to remember and thereby conditions his mind for positive response. Thirdly, reading does not consist of manually following each line with finger or pencil, moving one's lips and pronouncing audibly or inaudibly the words from line to line.

WHAT READING IS

Reading is thinking. It "is to the mind," wrote Joseph Addison, "what exercise is to the body." Reading consists of extracting, weighing, comparing, balancing, and applying to experience, thoughts from the printed page. The almost universal attitude is that having begun to read in the first years of elementary school, the job is finished. This is not true. Goethe was so right.

Read this paragraph taken from Roman history.

> When the evil Tarquin kings of Rome were banished, Lucius Junius Brutus was elected one of the two first consuls, in the year 509 B.C. His two sons entered into a conspiracy to restore the Tarquins. Their father judged them guilty of treason; he sentenced them to death and they were executed in his sight.

A poor reader reads the paragraph as part of an assignment in history. He is prepared to assure his teacher that Lucius Junius Brutus became consul in 509 B.C. Perhaps he has looked consul up in the dictionary. He can tell the history teacher that this father had two sons; that they were guilty of treason; that the father sentenced them and saw them executed.

The good reader seizes the main ideas, the date, which is not of primary importance, may be forgotten, but what is seen is a man who has driven from Rome an evil reigning house. Here is a man with a keen sense of right and wrong—just the kind of man you admire; just the kind of person you respect and honor. Rather than see evil triumph, he would see his own sons die; would, in fact, condemn them to death himself! Think of it! Would your father, acting as judge, condemn you thus if you were guilty of betraying your country? If he would not, is he weak? Think how the father must have felt when he condemned his sons and then saw them die. How would your father feel under such circumstances? Could you possibly be guilty of betraying your country? Would you surely stand for what is right? All this and much more flashes through the mind of the intelligent student as he reads about Lucius Junius Brutus. An intelligent, responsive reader of history might not make much of a grade when tested on Lucius Junius Brutus. But the responsive reader would feel good afterwards.

The exercise of reading and thinking is an extremely mental-visual psychological process, difficult to learn, impossible to a degree of efficiency without continued conscientious effort, but capable of improvement throughout one's lifetime. Reading is thinking, it is a search, it is a challenge; and when done successfully, it is an adventure which involves two persons—the reader and the author. The reader must carry on a silent conversation with the author, asking what is being said, questioning reasons, and approving or disapproving of the manner in which the material is presented. Reading is never passive acceptance. It is an energy-absorbing activity, requiring movement of mind, and sometimes heart, out to meet the mind of the author and to grasp the meaning of another's thoughts. "It is," says A. B. Herr, "a two-way process; the reader must give in order to receive."

READING IS PLANNING

The development of the ability to study effectively results to a great degree from the ability to read with sufficient skill and understanding. Most scholastic problems have the lack of skill in reading as their basis. Consequently, successful students plan their reading approach and execution as thoroughly as all other learning processes.

The good reader begins with three objectives that are kept in mind while reading: (1) to concentrate on what is being read, and this to the exclusion of such faults as making reading a part-time job, trying to read without thinking, without sufficient background and vocabulary, and without sufficient mechanical skill; (2) to remember as much as possible, and to convince oneself that what is read *is* to be remembered; and (3) to apply or associate what is read to personal experience. Only this makes memory possible, and turns knowledge into wisdom.

The good reader also plans the type of approach. The three general types of reading are: (1) skimming, (2) careful reading, and (3) intensive reading. The nature of the work and what is desired will determine the type to be used. Skimming is used to find a specific fact, to get the gist of a thesis, or to pick the most relevant ideas—such as topic sentences, introductory and concluding paragraphs—and form them into a composite theme. Skimming should be practiced on most material assigned for reading beyond the textbook.

Careful reading presupposes an awareness of what to look for, and is aimed at finding the main topics, fixing them in mind, and choosing significant details which supplement the main topics. This type of reading would be used for some textbook reading assignments and much background reading in preparation of themes, term papers, etc.

Intensive reading is the type of reading, demanding total concentration, used in mastering word problems, technical and documentary material, definitions, and other textbook material which is cumulative and cannot be missed. Any material requiring memorization is read intensively. All intensive reading is more effective if it can be done at short intervals rather than one long gruelling session.

Improvement in reading is also only effective when it is planned, and the reader who wishes to improve does all reading as practice for improvement in three areas: (1) to develop a keen awareness of what to look for; (2) to improve comprehension; and (3) to increase the speed of reading by reducing the number of eye fixations per line.

Changing your bad habits to good ones may be discouraging to you at the beginning of your practice. There will be a period when you find that the attempt to improve only confuses you. Once you start practicing for improvement, do not go back to the old habits. The practice for improvement in reading begins with the sentence and ends with the chapter. The progressive mastery of each will make your study easier and the results more gratifying.

READING THE SENTENCE

Very few ideas are expressed in single words. Therefore it is important to start reading groups of words (phrases) if you wish to improve your reading. Note the sentence below:

> The art of study is composed of a small amount of information
> and a tremendous amount of practice.

If you read the sentence word by word you have to go back to get the meaning. Now read the sentence by phrases: *The art of study is composed—of a small amount of information—and a tremendous amount of practice.* There are seventeen words in the sentence, but there are only three ideas. When you reduce the things to be fixed in your mind from seventeen to three, you make the sentence easy to understand and no time is wasted going back and putting the words together.

When you begin to practice reading for ideas, you will find yourself looking at groups of words in the sentence. These pauses of the eye in moving across the page are called fixations. If your eye picks out each word, you must begin your practice by trying to see two words at once, and so on until you are seeing five or six related words at a fixation. This will take time. You will spend thousands of hours reading during your lifetime. One year of serious practice, training your eyes to take in more at each fixation, will reward you for the rest of your life. You will be reading your English, science, history and other subjects day after day; make each reading assignment serve a dual purpose. Make the preparation of each reading assignment a practice in grouping ideas and gaining longer fixations. If you will attend to the ideas instead of individual words, your reading span will become wider and your understanding and speed will become greater.

READING THE PARAGRAPH

A paragraph is supposed to represent a unit of thought. You can be sure of this, however, only in expository writing—that is, writing that explains. Most textbooks follow rigidly the unit of thought for each paragraph.

The first or second sentence in a well-written paragraph is usually the topic sentence. It gives the topic of the paragraph. Having read the following topic sentence, you would know what the paragraph is about. *There were four important results—of the Persian wars—that affected the whole future—of the western world.* You read the topic sentence by ideas and fixations, and when you finish you know what the ideas are. If you read it word by word, you would not know.

The last sentence in a well-written paragraph is a summary sentence or a transitional sentence. The summary sentence tells you at a glance what the paragraph has said. If the last sentence of the paragraph is a transitional sentence, it leads you into the next paragraph. That is, it shows the relationship between the paragraph just finished and the one you are about to read.

Between the topic sentence and the summary sentence, the thought unit of the paragraph is explained. From the topic sentence given above the paragraph would develop, giving fully the four results of the Persian wars that affected the future of the western world.

Since a paragraph contains a unit of thought, it is the business of the reader to find and understand that thought. This cannot be accomplished by word reading. It is only accomplished by phrase-reading the sentences for understanding and uniting the ideas in the sentences to form a unit of thought. The poor reader looks at the three hundred words that make up the paragraph; the good reader looks for, and finds, the unit of thought upon which the paragraph is built. You could not get a good idea of how a house looks by going from board to board looking at each nail. Practice examining paragraphs deliberately to improve your reading. You can, with practice, become an expert at locating main thoughts.

There is one chief reason why the reader does not find main thoughts and that is chiefly caused by a simple lack of training. If you are reading words or pages only because they were assigned, and looking for nothing in particular, you will find just that. If you practice reading paragraphs as described above, you will find yourself understanding them better, and doing your reading assignments in half the time it once took you to assemble a mass of confused word distortions.

READING THE CHAPTER

In mastering the reading of the chapter or assignment, the preliminary is of primary importance. As a matter of fact, the reader could probably speak more intelligently about the lesson or chapter after a well-executed five-minute preliminary survey than after an hour's misguided reading that would result in scraps of information and a multitude of word distortions. Five steps are necessary in making a preliminary survey of your reading assignment. They will save you much time and afford much insight.

1. Try to determine from looking at the chapter title what will be explained in the chapter. If you can anticipate what is to be explained, you are preparing in your mind the background necessary for successful reading and understanding. The ideas you form from thinking around and ahead of the chapter title condition your mind for active thinking as you read.

2. If you are beginning a book, study the table of contents carefully. You can also use the table of contents for any assignment to determine how a particular chapter fits into the general topic of the book. This is important because no chapter of the book can be understood apart from the book as a whole.

3. Look over the chapter title and then the section titles. Chapters in textbooks usually do not contain more than four or five main divisions represented by individual headings. It is easy to remember the four or five main divisions, and they tell you what you are going to read about. If you start to read the details you may never know what the chapter is about.

4. Now that you know the title of the chapter and the main divisions, read carefully the subheadings or paragraph headings. Having read these carefully, you have in mind the fundamental organization of the ideas that will be developed in the chapter.

5. Most books are written with two or three introductory paragraphs for each chapter, and at least one good concluding paragraph. Now read these. The introductory paragraph will give you a composite picture of the material in the chapter, and the concluding paragraph will sum up the chapter for you.

When you have finished the preliminary survey, you have used between five and ten minutes. Now you can read ideas with understanding because you know what you are reading and what you expect to get out of what you read. The preliminary survey is of first importance, but there are three important additional steps in reading the chapter or assignment.

The second important step in reading the chapter or assignment is to read for ideas. Read each sentence by phrases. Note the topic and summary sentences. At the end of each section stop and review the ideas to yourself. If the section is long, you can summarize the ideas at the end of each paragraph.

The third important step in mastering the chapter is to reread those sections or paragraphs that you do not recall as you check back over the topic headings. Here is the practice that will help you discover your weak points.

The fourth important step in reading the chapter for complete mastery is to sum up the chapter in your mind; or better yet, reduce the chapter to a brief summary paragraph in your notebook. If you are required to outline, the outline automatically becomes the fourth step.

BAD PRACTICES IN READING

1. *Too many eye fixations.* For pleasure-type reading you should make only two or three fixations per line; for work-type reading you need from three to five.

2. *Regression.* Regression is going back to pick up omitted words or phrases, or merely going back from habit—the habit having been formed by daydreaming while you thought you were reading.

3. *Lip reading.* If you move your lips when you are reading, you are a word reader.

4. *Failure to use a dictionary.* Read with your dictionary close at hand. Use it to get the meaning of a difficult word.

5. *Not looking for something.* Whenever you read look for something definite. Keep your mind on the idea you are seeking.

PRACTICES FOR BETTER READING

1. *Expect to remember what you read.* Many students start by preparing their minds for passively going over material, because they tell themselves they will not remember. Do not be afraid to say to yourself, "I expect to remember this; I am going to remember it."

2. *Know the purpose for which you are reading.* Start by clearly understanding what it is you are looking for, and whether skimming, careful, or intensive reading will be required to accomplish your purpose.

3. *Read for ideas—not words.* Only thoughts have value; words are only symbols. Practice reading phrases rather than words. Read for the topic and its related details, not for details alone.

4. *Practice to increase the span of eye fixations.* Self-evaluate your span of concentration and use definite reading periods to test improved speed of reading. Fifteen-minute periods are most workable for many students. It is greatly to your advantage to increase your speed, for tests prove conclusively that fast readers remember more of what they read than slow readers.

5. *Practice summarizing rules, paragraphs, sections, and chapters quickly in your own words.* Ask yourself what questions are possible as you make a preliminary survey, and when you have finished answer your own questions and any others you think your teacher may ask. A question should always accompany your reading.

Improvement Chart for Reading Speed		
15-Minute Periods	History or Science Book	Fiction Book
1st period	Number of pages ____	Number of pages ____
2nd period	Number of pages ____	Number of pages ____
3rd period	Number of pages ____	Number of pages ____
4th period	Number of pages ____	Number of pages ____
5th period	Number of pages ____	Number of pages ____
6th period	Number of pages ____	Number of pages ____

NOTE: Make a duplicate chart for four practice periods per week. Plan to use the above chart to record your weekly average for the six weeks' practice.

REVIEW QUESTIONS

1. What are the several things which reading is not?
2. What are the three objectives of a good reader?
3. Name and explain the uses of the three types of reading.
4. Improvement in reading must always concern itself in three areas. Name them.
5. What are the four steps in the mastery of a chapter or reading assignment?

Developing A Vocabulary

Words are the only things that last forever.

— WILLIAM HAZLITT

The coldest word was once a glowing new metaphor.

— THOMAS CARLYLE

I gave them letters joined in words—the Mother of all arts.

— AESCHYLUS *(Prometheus's gift to man)*

INTEREST MEASUREMENT TEST

1. Do you keep a dictionary within reach as you read?
2. Do you use it when you come upon an unfamiliar word?
3. Do you read everything the dictionary says about a word?
4. Do you notice its origin and mentally list it alongside another word of the same origin?
5. When, in conversation, a person uses a pleasing and unusual word, do you have an urge to say, "My! What a good word for that particular use!"?

THE EXCITEMENT OF WORDS

The person who reads intelligently enjoys the very important added product of an improved vocabulary, for the proper pursuit of reading, sometimes even without it being consciously evident, is always increasing one's knowledge of words and the uses to which they may be put in order to gain a clearer understanding of what is read. Better use of words enables you to say more understandably what you wish to say.

There are approximately 600,000 words in the English language. Tests indicate that many persons know only a few thousand words, and worse, that some students reach college age with a working knowledge of only a few hundred. Words are the tools of thinking. Without these tools you cannot understand what is communicated to you; neither can you effectively communicate your thoughts to others.

Your capacity for thorough work in any subject (mathematics, English, science, etc.) depends largely upon your ability to master and use the fundamental vocabulary of the subject. Each subject, each area of study, has its fundamental vocabulary. You will find that the good students of the subject keep notebooks in which they write unfamiliar words and their meanings. This is more than a good practice; it is absolutely necessary if your aim is to master the subject.

Mental laziness and a limited vocabulary are usually bedfellows in the same brain. Handling words is like painting in that one must be able to distinguish between shades of meaning in words, as shades of color in painting, if the work at hand is to represent any measure of success. To know and understand the denoted and the connoted meaning of words that come upon in conversation and reading is to increase our ability to measure thought and improve our appreciation of man's greatest invention—speech.

Excitement and fascination trail the history of our 600,000 words, for each was in the beginning a stroke of genius. And according to Emerson, each "was once a poem." Uttering a single word is to strike a note on the keyboard of the imagination that vibrates backward in time so many thousands of years that any speculation on its origin is mere conjecture.

How many aeons our remote ancestors gestured and grunted to bring words finally into existence lies beyond the ability of the imagination to measure. Only about five thousand years ago a critical level of achievement was reached—man learned to scratch symbols on stones and clay. He had learned to write his words. By a magical stroke of genius a word became a tool for calling up memory and beauty to the mind. It made possible the exchange of ideas and impressions between individuals. As time passed, awkward combinations of words were made, and then from some primitive heart there welled up an emotional urge and words were put into rhythmic form—poetry was born. Words had reached the greatest use to which they can be put; as Coleridge said, "Poetry is the best words in the best order."

PRACTICES FOR WORD STUDY

Four simple and fascinating practices will bring you to a full realization of what an interesting study words can really become. First, you must learn to be aware of words you do not know; second, you must study the unfamiliar word in its relationship to the words used with it to determine its meaning; third, you must learn word parts and word families; and fourth, you must be willing to look up the meaning of words in a dictionary. We will take each practice separately and investigate its value to you.

1. *You must learn to be aware of words you do not know.* Below are lists of words picked from the beginning chapters of three textbooks. Do you know the exact meaning of the ten words in each list? You may have been using these words almost daily.

English	Mathematics	History
relative	ratio	reform
connective	circumference	confederacy
modify	measure	magistery
agreement	annually	anarchy
theme	theorem	theory
enunciate	equivalent	enfranchise
declarative	denomination	demagogue
reference	radical	radical
faulty	fraction	faction
phrase	proportion	phase

Perhaps the above lists will make you realize that day after day you pass over words whose meanings are unfamiliar, and, if you were to know them, your work would be much easier. At the front or back of each of your textbooks you should have a basic vocabulary for that particular course.

2. *You must study the word in relationship to the words with which it is used, and the way in which it is used.* Each unfamiliar word you meet should be studied in its context. Make the best appraisal you can of its meaning and then see whether the sentence makes sense when your meaning is applied.

You must apply this practice also to familiar words which have many meanings. Note the uses of the word "run" in the sentences below.

The boy will run home.

The boat runs to Boston.

He runs up big bills.

He had a close run in the election.

The dog had the run of the house.

He runs his business well.

The play had a long run.

In the sentences which follow see if you can tell the meaning of the underlined words by the context:

The crowd enjoyed the play; there followed several minutes of wholehearted <u>applause</u>.

The lion is a <u>carnivorous</u> animal living on animals it kills and carrion it finds in the jungle.

As was their custom, the <u>itinerant</u> workers did not remain long in the valley.

Learning the meaning of words from the context is a practice which will aid you in remembering the word. However, if you are not detective enough to find its true meaning, check with your dictionary.

3. *You must learn word parts and word families.* There are three word parts which you must be able to recognize: root words, prefixes, and suffixes. Recognizing a familiar part of a word that is unfamiliar may bring its meaning to you. Many English words have come from Latin or Greek. For example, the Latin word *manus,* meaning hand, serves as the root word in our words manual, manufacture, manuscript. The Latin word *ped,* meaning foot, serves as the root word for pedal, pedate, pedometer, pedicel, pedestal, pedestrian, peddler. The Latin word *porto,* meaning to carry, is the root word for port, portfolio, portage, portable, porter. Thus it is plain that a knowledge of word families and root words makes it easier to understand the meaning of many more words.

Another word part that must be readily recognized is the prefix. The prefix consists of one or more syllables that are attached to the word root and modify the meaning of the word. Below are given the most commonly used Latin and Greek prefixes and their meanings. If you know these, the meaning of many words will be made clear without the use of a dictionary.

Latin Prefixes

Prefix	Meaning	Example
a, ab	from, away	avert, abstain
ad, af, at	to	adhere, affix, attain
ante	before	antedate
circum	around	circumnavigate
con, cor	with, together	convene, correspond
contra, counter	against	contradict, counteract
de	from, down	descend, debase
di	apart	divert, divorce
dis	not	disagree, dissuade
e, ex	out of, from	eject, exit
extra	beyond	extravagance
in	not	inappropriate
im	in, not	import, impossible
ir	not	irresponsible
per	through	permeate, percolate
post	after	postpone, posterity
pre	before	predict, precede
pro	for, forth	pronoun, procession
re	back, again	recall, revive
sub, subter	under	subordinate, subterfuge
super	over, above	supervise
tra	beyond	traverse
trans	across	transport

Greek Prefixes

Prefix	Meaning	Example
a, an	without	atheist, anarchist
ambi	both	ambidextrous
amphi	around	amphitheater

ana	thought	analysis
ant, anti	against	antonym, antipathy
apo	from	apology
cata	down	catacomb, cataract
dia	through	diameter, diagnoses
hyper	above, over	hypercritical
hypo	under	hypodermic
meta	beyond	metaphysical
mono	one	monologue
para	similar	parable, parody
peri	around	perimeter
poly	many	polygon
syn	with	syndicate, synonym

The third word part which must be understood is the suffix. Suffixes come at the end of a word, and they, like prefixes, change the meaning of the word. Below are listed the commonly used suffixes.

Suffix	Meaning	Example
able	that may be, worthy of	movable
ible	that may be, worthy of	digestible
ac	pertaining to, the nature of	cardiac
al	pertaining to, the nature of	national
ial	pertaining to, the nature of	facial
ance	state of being	abundance
ence	state of being	obedience
ant, ent	one who, that which	servant, student
er, or	one who	teacher, sailor
ful	full of	hopeful, helpful
ish	having the quality of	boorish, mannish
ity	the quality of	ability, humility
ive	one who, that which	executive
less	without	voiceless, sleepless

ly	like	manly, cheerfully
ness	state of	goodness, holiness
ous	full of	anxious, joyous
ry	state of	rivalry, ministry

If you are familiar with the three word parts, you will find that many words once strange to your vocabulary will come into it without much trouble. In the sentence *Cotton was not an importable commodity until 1872* you have never seen the word *importable* but the three parts will tell you: *port* meaning to carry, *im* meaning in, *able* meaning worthy of, and you have "worthy of being carried in." Thus you understand that cotton could not be imported until 1872.

Along with the practice of studying root words and their parts, you should be able to recognize syllables so that you can make the parts stand out. Here are some of the simple rules for dividing words into syllables; these rules are not conclusive but they can aid greatly in helping you know words:

a. There are as many syllables in a word as there are vowels, except when two vowels are sounded as one or when the final *e* is silent.
   Example: dog, look, home

b. Consonants usually go with the following vowels.
   Example: se-cret, so-lo

c. If the accent is on the first syllable, the following consonant is usually included in the first syllable.
   Example: pal-ace

d. Consonants are split if they cannot be blended in speaking.
   Example: pic-nic, al-fal-fa

e. Double consonants are split.
   Example: col-lege, sil-ly

f. Prefixes and suffixes remain separate syllables.
   Example: re-turn-ing, in-for-ma-tion

4. *The fourth practice for learning the meaning of new words is to use your dictionary.* Here are some things you should know about using your

dictionary: (1) The two words printed at the top of the page are the first and last words on the page. Noting these at a glance can save you going up and down the columns of words, looking for a word that is not on the page. (2) The word is divided into syllables. Usually a (·) separates the syllables. (3) The pronunciation is indicated by accent marks and the sound spelling of the word. For example, documentary (dok yoo men ta ri). All accent marks are explained in one of the beginning sections of the dictionary. These should be reviewed, along with other introductory material, although you probably first made its acquaintance long ago in elementary school. (4) The parts of speech are usually shown in italic or boldface type—*n., v., adj., adv.* for noun, verb, adjective, or adverb. (5) The derivation follows the abbreviation (G) Greek, (L) Latin, (AS) Anglo-Saxon, etc., indicating the language from which the word has come down to us. (6) The definitions are next; the most common uses are given first. (7) Most entries conclude with one or more synonyms. Some also give antonyms.

Few people avail themselves of the complete program for word study offered by the dictionary. Many use it only to check spelling. Some use it hurriedly for word meaning, usually reading only the first definition. Those who appreciate words, strive to master their use, and add beauty and understanding to their speech and writing, omit nothing, measuring carefully both meaning and synonym for the most effective use. Only when used in this manner can the dictionary provide an avenue of improvement.

The dictionary habit can be made doubly successful if accompanied by a degree of honest and humble confession—the admission that many of the words used daily are known by sight, but are really not known in such a way as to be useful as a tool of learning.

EIGHT RULES FOR VOCABULARY IMPROVEMENT

1. Practice examining words that you see every day. Do you really know what they mean? Would your lessons be easier if you did?
2. Know the difference between denotation and connotation as regards

meaning. Note the many meanings of some very ordinary words.

3. Put a fundamental vocabulary in each textbook, listing the words that you use in that particular course.

4. Keep a list of new words you meet. Review the words often, until they are a working part of your vocabulary.

5. Try to figure out the meaning of strange words from the context of the sentence.

6. Learn word parts and word families. Remember root, prefix, and suffix.

7. Use the dictionary as a final check. Use it wisely by studying all it tells about a word.

8. Put each new word to work, so that it will quickly become a regular part of your thinking, writing, and speaking.

REVIEW QUESTIONS

1. Explain the statement "each word was in the beginning a miracle."

2. Give some of the many reasons why "speech" is man's greatest invention.

3. What are the four practices which can improve both interest in words and your vocabulary?

4. What are the seven things that dictionaries ordinarily tell about a word?

5. Write the eight rules for vocabulary improvement.

Putting Ideas in Order

Even a very good idea out of order is usually discarded as waste.

📖

In school and in life the well-wrought Plan for a day or a
speech is the blueprint for success.

INTEREST MEASUREMENT TEST

1. Do you pencil in a route to follow on a road map before you start a trip?
2. Do you outline a theme before you start to write it?
3. Do you believe that a half hour spent in planning may save five to ten times that in working time?
4. Do you believe that any work can be more effectively carried out through proper planning and improved perspective?
5. Has it ever occurred to you that the way to learn the most with the least effort is to get the thing to be learned in manageable form?

THE FUNCTION OF OUTLINES AND SUMMARIES

Much of the work you do in school will need to be put into manageable form. The outline and the summary are the principal methods for reducing your work to a workable mass for learning and a proper perspective for understanding. Both contribute to reducing quantity material to condensed quality. Both assist the learner in graphically picturing the structure and basic meaning of what has to be learned. Both aim at clarity and compactness—two of the most beneficial of all aids to learning.

When you were very young you were probably given a box of blocks which when put together made a single toy or picture, or perhaps you had a toy which was already assembled but certain parts were detachable and you spent much time taking these off and replacing them. You were getting your first experience in putting ideas in order.

Thinking arises from puzzlement. (We puzzle over a problem, a condition, a series of ideas that constitute a topic.) Much of your school work, therefore, takes the form of thought puzzles. The outline is used to solve thought puzzles. The summary is used to bring into total perspective, as though you moved backward to see the whole forest from looking at each individual tree.

OUTLINING

Outlining may best be defined as *a practical means of putting things in their proper perspective and order.* In making an outline, you first choose your perspective or point of view. (You will begin with the largest and go to the smallest, you will go from east to west, from detail to conclusion—induction—or from generalization to the specific—deduction.) The word *things* has significant meaning in the definition of outlining, for arranging things is outlining—laying out the parts of a boat, lining up dogs at a kennel show, etc. Words are only symbols used to represent ideas, and of course the ideas represent things—be they abstract (happiness, sorrow, etc.) or concrete (stones, states, or people). Outlining is a creative exercise demanding thought and precision, a learning process that will be used often in your formal education and, to a greater extent, in business or professional life thereafter. The practice of outlining is also one of the basic aids in the development of good study methods, for it teaches the art of selecting and distinguishing between the important and the unimportant. The form has been standardized over a period of long usage and does not lend itself to variation.

Title

I. Main Topic
   A. Subtopic
   B.
II. Main Topic
   A. Subtopic
   B.
   C.
      1.
      2.
         a.
         b.
            1)
            2)

The indentation is to the right, and always to a specific point. The subtopic symbol A. is placed directly under the first letter of the first word in the topic above. All topics of equal rank are directly below and above each other. A period is placed after each symbol until the parenthesis in the fifth step down. A well-organized outline begins with the main topic and ends with the smallest contributing, or subordinate, idea or detail.

Title: The Classical Tradition

I. Greek Poetry
II. Latin Poetry
III. English Poetry
   A. Epic poetry
   B. Lyric poetry

  C. Dramatic poetry
    1. Marlowe's dramatic poetry
    2. Shakespeare's dramatic poetry
      a. Comedies
      b. Tragedies
        1) Richard II
        2) Julius Caesar

Title: The History of Early Law

I. Definition of Law
II. Evolution of Law
  A. Mutual respect
  B. Community tradition
III. Great Lawgivers
  A. Hammurabi
  B. Moses
  C. Solon
  D. Justinian

Title: Sentences

I. Kinds
  A. Declarative
  B. Interrogative
  C. Imperative
  D. Exclamatory
II. Forms
  A. Simple
  B. Complex
  C. Compound
  D. Compound-complex

Topics in your textbooks are usually arranged in their proper relationships, so that the actual outlining of a textbook is not difficult.

The greatest problem in outlining your textbook will be learning to discriminate between the important and the superfluous. Most students put too much in the outline. You must learn to pick out vital facts, and facts that assist or complement the vital facts. You must learn to identify the repetitions, illustrations, comparisons, transitions, etc.—and leave them out of your outline.

Establishing the relationship between these ideas you are going to put into a theme requires the added skill of putting the puzzle together without first having seen what its form is. For example, you suddenly find yourself with an animal farm. You have six animals—buffalo, horse, antelope, sheep, moose, and cow—and you have two pens. What animals will you put in the first pen, and what animals in the second pen?

Animal Farm

I. Domestic Animals
    A. Horse
    B. Cow
    C. Sheep
II. Wild Animals
    A. Moose
    B. Buffalo
    C. Antelope

You would not think of arranging them in any other manner; you have used the only practical arrangement possible. As in arranging your animal farm, so in outlining; you aim at the only practical arrangement of ideas possible.

The practical arrangement of ideas is influenced by several possible methods of order. They may be referred to as the order of outlines. The guiding principle behind all orders is, of course, logical arrangement. The several others are:

1. Time order
2. Mechanical order
3. Arbitrary order
4. Place order
5. Numerical order
6. Alphabetical order

If you were outlining a person's life you would doubtless start with his birth and end with his death. This is time, or chronological, order. How to make a boat would be outlined by mechanical order, from the first steps in building to the finished product. Arbitrary order is arrangement according to one's own desires, but reasonableness (rationality) should be of first consideration in deciding on arrangement. In outlining a day's work you would put first the things that had to be done. At the end of the day would come those things which are not imperative, but which must be done sometime. Place order would be used in outlining directions for cleaning a house, for lining up prizewinning animals at a fair, etc. Alphabetical and numerical outlines fall into place in an arbitrary manner, but in most outlines the greater numerical factors come first. In listing the populations of the fifty states, the state with the greatest population would probably be first. In alphabetical order no problem arises; it is unlikely that you would start with Z and go to A.

Outlining requires precision; it develops the power to discriminate between the important and the *superfluous;* it disciplines the mind to orderliness; it teaches the art of planning, and whether the plan be for a vacation, for an attack upon an elephant, for a term paper, the answer to an examination question, or an intelligent verbal reaction, if the plan succeeds, it will first have been carefully outlines.

SUMMARIZING

A summary gives in condensed form the main ideas of a body of material. The ideas are usually presented in the order of the original text, but this is not an absolute requirement. A good summary does, however, follow the following rules: (1) No fundamental ideas are omitted. (2) No new ideas are introduced. (3) No general or editorial elements are attached to main ideas. (4) The point of view of the original text is maintained. (5) The summary is put in the writer's own vocabulary and not that of the original text.

Fundamentally the same as the summary just defined is the précis (French meaning precise and pronounced [*pray-see*]) form of condensing. In addition to the five requirements of a summary, the précis adds a sixth requirement as its name suggests. It follows precisely the order and proportion—part by part—of the original text; and undertakes to maintain something of the original tone without requiring the vocabulary of the text.

You will also encounter the word synopsis (Greek *syn*, together—and *opsis*, to see) in reference to summaries of stories or poems. A synopsis is a brief and general summary, picturing with much broader strokes than are permitted by summary or précis.

The ability to write a good summary will provide you with these advantages: (1) one of the best study methods for reviewing your work; (2) an improved ability to think and condense; (3) an aid to recalling the essentials of your work; (4) the skill to judge quickly between main points and contributing items; and, perhaps the most valuable aid of all, (5) the ability to organize and write smoother, more unified, and more complete answers on tests and examinations.

Indeed most summary writing during your school life will be either reviewing for, or answering, questions. Some students mistakenly practice putting down a group of unrelated sentences, expecting them to be accepted as a summary. They do not make a summary. An acceptable summary is a miniature composition. It begins with a topic sentence. It contains unity, coherence, and emphasis, as do all good compositions. Connection between sentences is indicated; and if more than a single paragraph, proper transition is required.

Summary writing starts as a challenge. Reducing sentences to phrases, phrases to meaningful words, will require practice and the study of summary material provided by reference books. But economy of words can become an important part of your learning, a time-saver, and also help improve your marks. The length of a summary will vary according to purpose and the requirements of your teachers. However, for your own review summaries, try to keep them below one-third the size of the original text. If after extensive practice, you can reduce them to one-fifth, it is all the better. A well-written summary is a test of how completely you have understood a paragraph, a chapter, an assignment, or a book—and how concisely and clearly you have been able to condense it without loss of meaning.

In the paragraph above, mention was made of studying summaries in reference books. Space prohibits examples of summaries here, but there is a storehouse of model outlines and summaries awaiting you in the reference books of your school library.

Start with a junior encyclopedia, such as *World Book, Junior Britannica,* or any that is available. Read the summarization of the history of your state or city. Read several biographies. Not carefully the division of topics, the choice of words, and the use of graphic material in dealing with population, industry, resources, etc. If there are one-volume encyclopedias on the reference shelf, compare the facts it presents with those of the ten-volume work.

Equally as valuable as seeing how material is summarized, is to learn what summaries exist ready at hand to help you. Are you enjoying your algebra class? Is the study of chemistry proving difficult for you? Are you confused about "Jacksonian Democracy" as it is presented in your textbook? Look up *algebra* in the encyclopedia. Here you will find the course, its principal parts, the methods of solving equations, and illustrations to clarify difficult problems. From a four-page summary your whole conception of the course may be changed. You may really understand for the first time what algebra is all about. Do the same for your chemistry. The enlightenment resulting from such brief inquiry can change both your attitude, your understanding, and your mark. Check "Jacksonian Democracy" in a junior encyclopedia, then a larger one, or an encyclopedia of history. It is so easy to learn if you bother to give a little thought to finding what you want.

Perhaps you have more than once been in a situation similar to the student who, reading Homer's *Iliad* in poetry translation, could not follow the thread of the story. After much persuasion he looked up the *Iliad* in an encyclopedia. There he found it summarized by books. Book II, which was causing the reader so much trouble, was summarized in nine lines; and the whole twenty-four books, the thread of the story plainly given, in three and a half pages. From this time on the student did not have to be persuaded to use the summaries available to him. He was able to read the *Iliad* and enjoy it. He discovered that the reference shelf in the library was filled with study aids, waiting to be used to clarify and save time.

Books of facts, general encyclopedias, encyclopedias of specific subjects—history, literature, science—all contain summarized material that can provide quick clarification. Atlases, handbooks, and dictionaries of all kinds beckon from the reference shelf in the library. The use of carbon 14 to explain that Cro-Magnon man's campfire in a cave in France burned 11,000 years ago sounds complicated and difficult. Look it up in a reference book. The whole process is summarized in half a column.

REVIEW QUESTIONS

1. Define outlining; tell in what way a summary may differ from précis writing.
2. What are the six orders of outlines? What principle always determines the order?
3. A good summary adheres to five specific requirements. Name them.
4. Summarizing offers practice in improving your ability in five areas of your school work. Name them.

5. Explain the several advantages of studying model outlines and summaries in reference books. Can you relate these advantages to Woodrow Wilson's definition of education as "education is knowing where to find what you want"?

7

Books and the Library

Education is knowing where to find what you want.
— WOODROW WILSON

When the destroyer comes, his first act is to burn the books.
— SIR THOMAS MORE

Books are the memory of mankind.

INTEREST MEASUREMENT TEST

1. Have you ever stopped to think what your life would be like if there were no books?
2. Accepting the definition of books as "the memory of mankind," is there a single greater factor that has influenced our existence as much as books?
3. Do you acquaint yourself with a book before you start to read or study it?
4. Which is the most important building in your town: the town hall, the church, or the library?
5. Has it ever occurred to you that the reference books in a library can in many ways make your studies easier and more meaningful?

WHAT BOOKS ARE

In an earlier chapter books were listed as one of the three basic tools of education. They are defined as "the memory of mankind." Man remains the only creature capable of recording his memory, and this accumulated memory—books—is that factor which (far more than any other) provided the bootstraps whereby man has been able to lift himself from the dark, fearful superstition and ignorance of savagery.

In books the accumulated knowledge of mankind is made available to you—to the last ripple on the sea of emotion and the faintest whisper of agony that has stirred the heart of the world, all that is dream and all that is real. Books are the chief source of life's enrichment over the centuries. They push back the boundaries of our ignorance, and open wide vistas of thought and history that reach beyond the incomplete and narrow experience of the generation of which we are a part, and we become a part of the whole human community in all time and in all places.

Books lead us realistically and rationally into the past and speculatively with vision, hope, and confidence into the future; they present cases from yesterday upon which we can formulate judgments today, and ideals for tomorrow; they stir us up and cause us to take a second look at things we have taken for granted. Books are, apart from the tireless effort and endless influence of a good teacher, the chief source of education, and through them you explore the richness of human experience and the wisdom of the ages. "Of all the inanimate objects, of all men's creations," wrote Joseph Conrad in his autobiography, "books are the nearest to us, for they contain our very thought, our ambitions, our indignations, our illusions, our fidelity to truth, and our persistent leaning towards error."

Have you ever stopped to think of what our world would be like without books? Sit quietly for ten minutes (time yourself) and try to think of as many things as you can that would not be available to you were it not for books. After this ten minutes you will never again feel the same about books. The textbooks you have perhaps felt you would be just as happy without, take on new meaning; they become a part of a treasure without which we might not be called "human."

HOW TO USE BOOKS

If you were going on a journey with a person, you would want to know as much as possible about your companion before you start. Why then do you accept the responsibility for spending days, weeks, or even months with a book without bothering to find out something about it before you start?

An excellent way to approach a book (and this includes your textbooks) is to ask yourself questions about the book and its parts. Why did the author write it? What are the author's qualifications? Does the table of contents suggest good organization of material? Is it sufficiently fitted to your needs—specific and specialized if it is a subject you know, general if it is a new subject you are just beginning to explore? What would you have done differently to make it more attractive? Could the title have been improved?

The parts of a book that should be noted when it is begun are: title, author, imprint, copyright, printings, foreword, preface, table of contents, list of illustrations, sometimes an introduction in addition to preface, usually a translator's note if book is translated from a foreign language, chapter titles, often subdivision heads, notes, appendices, sometimes defining or pronouncing glossaries, bibliography, and index. Of course, all these would not be found in a novel, but a well-written textbook would perhaps contain most of the parts, and all should be carefully studied.

A test question—What is the full title of your textbook and who is the author?—revealed that eight people out of thirty did not know the full title of a book they had been studying for four months, and seventeen of the thirty did not know the name of the author. When you begin a book, note the minor parts. If there is a note of information giving the qualifications of the author read it carefully. This, plus a thorough reading of the preface, should put you on a personal footing with the author.

Some books are arranged with chapter introductions—set in italics or small type. These should be carefully read after the chapter title itself. Frequently such a line or two will illumine the topic to be covered. In good translations of many classics, such as Homer, Dante, or Goethe, a brief survey of what the chapter contains is given as an aid to the reader; especially is this true of translations in poetry form. Some authors also make a point of introducing a chapter with a short, topical quotation from another writer. These, plus subdivision headings, illustration captions, footnotes, and end-of-chapter notes all require more than a passing glance for the reader who sets out to choose the best book, or acquaint himself with the book he has been assigned.

Perhaps the use you wish to make of a book, as seen in getting acquainted, can also best be determined by questions. Is this the book on the subject that I want? Is it too advanced or too elementary? What do I want to get out of it? What does it offer that will be valuable to me? These questions relate, of course, chiefly to work-type and nonfiction books. Your own personal tastes will prompt questions regarding fiction, poetry, and other reading for pleasure.

The reader with an alert intellectual curiosity will use each book to get just exactly what is wanted from it and no more, and will know first of all why it is being read. There are about four general reasons that cover the use of books: (1) to get information, (2) to improve ability to think, (3) for personal and professional development, and (4) for the sheer joy of reading. The person who is capable of wise judgment will get the best out of many books instead of everything out of a few. There are many dull books, not a few of which you will be condemned to read in the process of educating yourself in school and after. But if you know what you are looking for, and though the dullest book gives you only the smallest fraction of what you seek, anticipation generated from intellectual curiosity can remove the sting of boredom and often lead to discovery of more than you thought the book capable of offering.

"Light from two sources," says an old axiom, "is the way to get rid of shadows." This is so pointedly true in the use of books. Teachers often suggest to students who are finding a subject difficult and uninteresting that they read one or two general or related books on the subject. The results are usually what the teacher anticipates—renewed interest and new light (understanding). The student who hates biology reads a biography of the great naturalist Louis Agassiz or Charles Darwin's adventures on the scientific exploration of the South Seas aboard *The Beagle*, and biology becomes a favorite subject. A student who finds American history dull, and the textbook filled with one difficult maze of facts after another, reads Oscar Handlin's life of William Lloyd Garrison and two or three chapters from one of Dr. Samuel Eliot Morison's books. Here is the secret for bringing American history to life—use the book for the general reader first, then the textbook. Twice as much is learned with half the effort, and "light from two sources" has dispelled the shadows of dullness.

Students in a beginning Latin class thought it very strange that the class's first assignment was to read a little book about Romans entitled *Roman Panorama*.[1] They wondered later why so many students from other classes dropped Latin, while no one from their class did. The teacher knew. *Roman Panorama* gave a readable, entertaining picture of the everyday life and customs of the Romans. When the boys and girls met the first Latin words, they knew something about the people who had spoken them.

HOW TO USE THE LIBRARY

Knowing the parts of a book—title, author, publisher, date of publication, edition—is the first step toward finding what you want in the library. With this information you are prepared to enter and find

[1]Humphrey Grose-Hodge, *Roman Panorama*, The Macmillan Company, 1947.

whether or not the book you want is in the library. For this information you go to the Card Catalog.

The Card Catalog is not a catalogue in book form. It is rather a series of drawers labeled with letters of the alphabet. The card files are really an alphabetical index to the library. All cards are filed alphabetically, beginning with the first important word of the title—A, An, and The are omitted. In addition to the title card there is also an author and subject card. The title card is the quickest if you know what book you want. Subject cards are not included for fiction except for historical novels of recognized merit.

You cannot carry the file to the librarian to show her what book you want. You must write out (sometimes special forms are provided) the following information: (1) call number, (2) author's name, (3) title, (4) volume and edition, and (5) your own name.

There are two widely used systems of classification, the Dewey Decimal and the Library of Congress systems. The Dewey Decimal is the one you will probably use most often. It was developed at Amherst College in 1873, and catalogues all knowledge under *ten* divisions, each assigned a group of numbers.

Dewey Decimal System

Numbers	Main divisions	Subdivisions
000–099	General Works	Almanacs, encyclopedias, bibliographies, magazines, newspapers. Materials that cannot be narrowed to a single subject.
100–199	Philosophy	Logic, history of philosophy, systems of philosophy, ethics, and psychology.

200–299	Religion	Sacred writings (the Bible), mythology, history of religions, all religions, and theologies.
300–399	Sociology (Social Sciences)	Group dynamics, law, government, education, economics.
400–499	Philology (Study of Linguistics)	Dictionaries dealing with words (not of biographies), grammars, and technical studies of all languages.
500–599	Science (Subject and Theoretical)	Astronomy, biology, botany, chemistry, mathematics, physics, etc.
600–699	Applied Science (Useful Arts)	Agriculture, all types of engineering, business, home economics, medicine, nursing, etc.
700–799	Fine Arts (Professional and Recreative)	Architecture, painting, music, performing, sports, etc.
800–899	Literature	All types of literature— drama, essays, novels, poetry, etc.—in all languages of all countries.

900–999	History	All history, biography, geography, and travel, etc.

If you go to the section of the library shelving Applied Science, 600–699, you will see immediately that each subdivision is further divided. For example, 600–610 will have general books or collections dealing with applied science. Medicine will be classified under 610. Books on engineering will begin with 620 and be further broken down by smaller decimals. A glance at the history shelves will reveal that 900–909 are general works of history; 910 is geography; and so on by decimal subdivision. English is subdivided into literature of nations, then further catalogued. For example, English literature is 820; English poetry 821; English drama 822; and so on to 829.99. English poetry, 821, is further subdivided; 821.1 is Early English poetry; and so on to 821.9, each designating a specific period. A little observation will make it easy for you to find the exact spot in a particular section of the library where the subject you are interested in can be pinpointed.

The Library of Congress system of classification designates the main divisions of knowledge by letters instead of numbers. Subdivisions in the Library of Congress system are made by the addition of a second letter and whole numbers. No detailed explanation will be given of this system beyond the letter classification of knowledge.

Library of Congress System

Letter	Main Divisions
A	General Works
B	Philosophy and Religion
C	History—Auxiliary Sciences
D	History—Topography (except American)
E–F	American History—Topography
G	Geography—Anthropology

H	Social Sciences
J	Political Sciences
K	Law
L	Education
M	Music
N	Fine Arts
P	Language—Literature (nonfiction)
Q	Sciences
R	Medicine
S	Agriculture
T	Technology
U	Military Science
V	Naval Science
Z	Bibliography and Library Science
P–Z	Literature (fiction)

Fiction and Biography

Fiction and biography are usually arranged in a section set aside for each, and the cataloguing is usually simplified. This is always true of fiction. In the fiction section, the books are arranged alphabetically by the author's last name. In case of two or more books by the same author, they are shelved alphabetically by title. Some libraries use the classification symbol F or **Fic** plus the first letter of the author's last name.

Biography is usually classified by the letter **B** or number **92**. However, some libraries classify individual biography under **921** and collective biographies under the number **920**. The **B** and **92** classifications also carry the first letter of the last name of the person written about. Thus a biography of Abraham Lincoln would be designated $\frac{B}{L}$ or $92 \atop L$ Biographies are arranged on the shelf alphabetically by the last name of the person written about. In case of more than one biography written about the same person, arrangement is alphabetically by the author's name. Collective biographies are arranged alphabetically according to the author or compiler's name.

One of the most valuable and timesaving uses of the library for you can be the use of reference books: dictionaries, encyclopedias, atlases, almanacs of facts, handbooks, and dictionaries of biography and specialized subjects. Reference books provide a springboard from a mere name to a detailed study, for the reference books give the beginning of information but provide bibliographies for almost inexhaustible pursuit of further study on a topic. If you are just beginning a topic, do not be embarrassed to start your investigation in a junior encyclopedia; they are excellent for introductory study.

Anyone using a library today will probable be confronted with a computer storing all the bibliographical information formerly available on catalogue cards. Eventually, and sadly, all card catalogues will probably be discarded in favor of computer screens. The single advantage of the computer is its ability to (a) store vast amounts of information and (b) to sort this information in such a way as to make it easy and fast to locate primary and corollary sources. Any librarian will be glad to show you to use these machines.

REVIEW QUESTIONS

1. What are the parts of a book that should be observed in forming an acquaintance with the book?
2. What are some of the questions a beginning reader should ask about a book?
3. Condense into a paragraph the value of books to mankind.
4. Write a paragraph describing your conception of life if suddenly there were no books.
5. From the chapter "Putting Ideas in Order" relate two examples to show the great benefits which may be derived from the effective use of reference books.

8

Written Work

Reading makes a full man, conferences a ready man and writing an exact man. —FRANCIS BACON

The most valuable of all talents is that of never using two words when one will do. — THOMAS JEFFERSON

A word after a word after a word is power.
— MARGARET ATWOOD

INTEREST MEASUREMENT TEST

1. Do you follow specific instructions in all your written work—such as how the pages should be numbered, where your name should be written, how and where questions should be labeled, how the title should be located, whether or not a line is omitted between answers?
2. Can you think of several very important reasons why the seemingly little things noted in the first question should be carefully observed?
3. Do you have a sense of pride in the way you dress and look?
4. Do you like people to get a good first impression of you?
5. Are you proud of the appearance of a theme, a test paper, or a simple daily written assignment when you have finished it?

THE THING YOU HAVE TO SELL

The papers you are asked to write in school fall mainly in several groupings: daily written work, weekly or term papers, tests, and book reports. Of the several skills you will develop in educating yourself—listening, reading, speaking, thinking, and writing—the one which will give your teachers the widest range for measuring your ability and achievements will be your writing. It is also the skill which you will use without much help from the teacher, for most of your written work will be done in class to answer questions (and the teacher cannot help) or out of class when you are on your own.

Beyond the drills provided in the fundamentals—spelling, handwriting, punctuation and capitalization, structure and pattern, in your English classes—your ability and skill in writing will almost always be judged as a finished product. The judgment will fortunately, or unfortunately, affect what your teachers in every school subject think of your work; because it is in writing that you offer them what you have learned. Not only is your written work the measure of what you have learned, but it reveals more of your character, your willingness to pursue excellence or accept mediocrity, than perhaps any other of your school work. It is, in fact, the most important product that you have to sell. You sell it, not for dollars and cents, but for a grade. As with any other product, the quality product brings the quality price.

Written work is to impart information or develop thought. The *primary requirements* of all written work are that it be presented in: (1) an interesting, (2) mechanically correct, and (3) attractive manner. Of course, the quality of a group of problems or a word list is measured only by the degree of correctness and attractiveness; attractiveness being accomplished by neatness and arrangement.

No written work is complete until it is the neatest that can be done. Form, spelling, handwriting, punctuation, are all parts of the final product that must be given consideration whether the work be a sentence or two, or a term theme. Evaluate your own work, make a judgment of your own sense of pride concerning your work. Put your self in your teacher's place. How would you grade it for quality if you were the teacher?

To write well, you must think correctly. You cannot hope to write clearly unless you first have clearly in mind what you are going to write. Before you attempt to write anything, even the answer to the simplest question on a daily quiz, you must have something to say. Not all students are gifted with equal creative ability, but all are responsible in a very real way; it is indeed a moral obligation to carry out certain practices of intent and honesty. These may be called the basic obligations of all students toward written work, and they are three in number: (1) All are obligated to study sufficiently in order to have a working knowledge of the subject before beginning to write. (2) All are equally obligated to use all the skill they possess to convert this information into an interesting, coherent piece of writing. (3) All are obligated (and the seriousness of this obligation touches the very character of the student) to never try to pass off thoughtless, boring, and sloppily executed written work merely to get by.

HOW TO JUDGE QUALITY

Perhaps one of the best methods of producing quality writing is to always approach it with questions, and judge it by questions when it is written. Ask yourself the following questions about the next one- or two-sentence answers you write. Use these only as beginners, and add questions of your own. Make them progressively demanding until you feel that you have acquired the ability to sense and produce quality answers and to detect and avoid worthless quantity. Can I start my answer by restating the idea of the question and thereby make it easy for the reader to mark my paper? Will I carefully avoid using a pronoun to replace the subject of the question? Does this answer contain the fewest number of words possible to make a quality answer? Is this a generalization that does not answer the question, but a dishonest attempt to get by which the teacher will detect immediately? These four questions can change the nature of the answers you write for tests.

Perhaps you have had the experience of writing a paragraph and then remembering something you wish you had included; not too important, but significant enough to have added to the unity and contributed to the completeness of the thought. Asking questions *before* you write can save you much regret and rewriting. Since the paragraph requires definite pattern and structure, as well as content, the questions for it become doubly important. Use the following as beginners, but add your own: (1) Do I have a complete mental blueprint of what this paragraph is to contain? (2) What topic sentence do I want to convey the topic clearly to my reader? (3) What paragraph pattern will best develop the topic? (4) Will my arrangement of ideas lead naturally from main to supporting ideas? (5) Will my choice of words make my meaning clear? (6) Will this paragraph contain only the material necessary to picture the thought or answer completely? (7) Will it be judged as distinctive quality writing or muddled generalization whose only measure is quantity, and gradewise devoid of value? (8) Will my concluding statement (summary sentence) convince my reader of my ability to control, condense, and keep meaningful structure to the end?

It might surprise and even annoy you that a simple paragraph demands such planning. Perhaps incentive to undertake these practices may come from the realization that you will probably be marked on hundreds of single paragraph test answers before you finish your formal schooling. It might also be remembered that whether you write a two or ten thousand word theme, the total merit will be measured by the quality of the sentence, first, and the paragraph, next.

Excellence, like courtesy, manners, and thoughtfulness, has become somewhat old-fashioned from lack of use. Since you will hear "minimum requirement" and "permissible" so often to describe what is acceptable, we might pause to examine this beautiful word "excellence," lest it miss being a part of your vocabulary, or, more importantly, miss being a part of your philosophy of life.

"What is excellent is permanent," wrote Emerson. "But how does this relate to something as simple as the way I write a daily quiz paper?" you ask. Each paper you write confronts you with dealing poorly with yourself and producing the "minimum" or "permissible," or dealing wisely with yourself and producing "excellence."

RULES FOR IMPROVING WRITTEN WORK

1. *Put yourself in your teacher's place.* Is your paper as neat as the teacher wants it? Are the problems or questions spaced properly, or crowded together? What grade would you give for quality if you were grading it?

2. *Know why and what you are writing.* Read the instructions, questions, or topic carefully. Never start writing until you clearly understand what is to be done. Seventy percent of failing grades on papers are there because of carelessness, carelessness in form and order, or carelessness in reading instructions as to what was required before you started writing. Know what you are supposed to do before you start.

3. *Be specific and definite.* Your teacher is impressed by neatness, by conciseness, and accuracy. Use clear, simple English. Be sure you say what you mean. Don't dilute your thought with ineffective modifiers. Make every word count.

4. *Make your written papers improve your grades.* Students who turn in neat papers make fewer mistakes. If you run your letters together, never dot the i's, never bother with the form of your paper, you are a failure, and your teacher knows it.

5. *When a paper is returned, go over it very carefully.* Check the mistakes so as to avoid repeating them. Only a disinterested fool walks past the trash basket and throws away a paper that has just been returned. Your teacher has spent a great deal of time checking mistakes so that you will not make them on the very next paper you turn in. Take advantage of such help. Check your mistakes carefully.

6. *In writing a theme, plan before you write.* If you are allowed to choose the topic, narrow it sufficiently to give some definitiveness of treat-

ment. Do not try to describe in a two-page theme a topic that would need a book to develop.

7. *Make an outline.* Decide what the main topics are, and what their chronological, logical, or arbitrary place is in the theme. Decide what subtopics will be included. Do not put together a patchwork of ideas that will take longer to revise than it did to write. Outlining one or two themes will convince you that the outline saves time. The outline prevents you from making mistakes, omissions, blunders in selection and exclusion, contradictions. The outline insures proper proportion of parts. It helps you to discover important ideas. No one ever built successfully without a plan. No one ever writes successfully without an outline.

8. *Examine your outline carefully.* Ask yourself the following questions about the outline: (a) Does the outline move directly forward, without overlapping or omissions? (b) Is there a sensible proportion among the topics given? (c) Will the plan be clear to the reader after perusing the first paragraph? (d) Can I state the "message" of the theme in one clear sentence?

9. *When you start to write, write rapidly.* Rapid writing helps the flow of ideas. Your revision will have to deal only with errors in mechanics. The slow writer struggles for each word, ties simple matters into knots, and tangles sentences and constructions. The job of revision for the slow writer becomes a major one. Ideas must be untangled, and, for the most part, the entire job done again.

10. *Do not underestimate your task.* Good theme writing is not a simple job; it demands responsibility, skill, continued practices in clear thinking and pride in form. Words must be measured for precision and clarity. Modifiers must be questioned for value. The good theme will reflect the sincerity of the writer and win the reader's appreciation.

RESEARCH THEMES

As stated elsewhere, your teacher is impressed by conciseness and accuracy. Perhaps the research theme lends itself to this practice as much as any paper you will be asked to write. There is a great deal of difference between having to say something and having something to say. Writing a research theme is not a mountainous task if you have something to say. If you have read sufficiently and have taken notes properly, you should have an abundance of material at hand. A paper that contains real meat will not need bombast and hot air to make its merits evident. Most of the problems in research themes arise from lack of material. A few years ago a student came to me for help on a research theme. He was writing on superstitions that have lasted down through history in one form or another. That evening I spent about three hours going through the writings of Herodotus to find early superstitions. I marked them very carefully and gave them to the boy. He returned the book after one class period. "You haven't finished?" said I. "Yes, Sir. I only needed two more pages to get my two thousand words." I hope he failed. He had copied enough words to put the beginning of his paper at the end.

Below are a number of suggestions for improving your research themes:

1. Before you start gathering information, write in one short paragraph what your objective or objectives for the theme are. Don't get halfway through your theme and decide you approached the subject from the dullest possible angle.

2. Do ample background reading and gather plenty of information before you start to write. It is the accomplishment of a real scholar to handle material on a large scale, and give it pointed clarity by condensation.

3. Take notes on your research in the form best adapted to the subject.
   a. Notes should be comparatively short.
   b. Notes should carefully respect all quotations.
   c. Notes should be on one side of 3 x 5 index cards or on one side of loose-leaf notebook paper.
   d. When you take notes leave space between parts of material to add if necessary.

    e. Notes should include your thoughts on material as you read.

    f. Include your bibliographic references on your notes so as to simplify the making of a bibliography when the paper is finished.

4. Before you start your theme, arrange your notes in the most sensible order; that is, the order which will make writing easiest for you. If it is a fact theme, time order will probably serve you best. If it is a thought theme, inductive reason order will probably provide the best pattern.

5. Make an outline from your notes before you start writing the theme. An outline always saves time. See rule number 8 above for testing your outline.

6. Make your theme show by its content that you have read widely. Too many students use one source book, and then falsify the bibliography by copying from the card catalogue in the library.

7. Make your bibliography speak for the worth of your paper. Here is probably how a bibliography for a theme on *The Peculiar Habits of the Mockingbird* would look:

> Audubon, John J., *Birds of America*, The Macmillan Company, 1946, chap. IV.
>
> Devoe, Allan, "Our Feathered Neighbors," *Nature Magazine*, October, 1951, pp. 21–39.
>
> Hausman, Leon A., *American Birds*, Halcyon House, 1944, chap. IX.
>
> Murray, James, *Wild Wings*, John Knox Press, 1947, chaps. V and VII.
>
> Pough, Richard M., *Birds of the South*, The Macmillan Company, 1941.

8. Footnotes should be included to give author, title, and page of quotations or ideas used. For example:

> John Kieran, "Nature's Mimics," *The National Geographic,* June, 1953. This article gives many more examples of the collecting habits of the mockingbird.

The above footnote would provide your reader with a wider survey of this very interesting habit of the mockingbird. If this were the first footnote in your theme, you would have designated it by the arabic numeral [1] at the end of your paragraph dealing with habits, and the same designation would precede the footnote at the bottom of the page.

9. Use correct English. Your paper must be free of mechanical errors. A paper is worthless if there are mistakes in spelling, punctuation, diction, etc.

10. There is no substitute for neatness. Your whole effort is measured by the pride you take in your own production.

BOOK REPORTS

Another kind of written composition that will require all the good practices of thought, outlining, mechanical correctness and neatness, plus the ability to deal with a special type of material, is the book report in which you will demonstrate how well you have read and understood books you are assigned to read.

A book report is primarily a description or account of the contents of a book, or a synopsis of its story. But like all other related reading and writing activities, a book report is also an exercise in thinking—thinking of the content of the book as it relates to your own experience, and then putting certain thoughts about the content into form which will give the reader the picture you wish to convey.

There are no special rules or form for writing book reports. Your teacher will probably give you a format to follow. This will include where to put the title, author, date of publication, and probably what to use in the way of character study, thread of story, etc.

If the book report is short, it is best to relate the story by using the reporter's four w's—who, where, when, and why. And even the brief report should contain a statement of the format, for an appreciation of the physical appearance of a book reflects a spiritual feeling for what books contain. Why you liked or disliked the book should not be stated editorially as a blank positive or negative statement. The last element in the brief report should deal with the main character or characters. The subtlety by which you deal with the characters should reveal your feeling about the book. The impression created should be

sufficiently graphic so as to create an atmosphere of personal relationships—you were introduced to these characters, or character; you
spoke with them, you saw them in action. From this your reader will
be able to judge how much you liked or disliked the book. The short
report here being considered would probably range, according to
your teacher's requirements, between one and two hundred words.

The long book report, up to four or five hundred words, also
deals with format, time, place, action, and characters, but goes beyond these. In the long report, the four elements of any piece of writing can also be given some attention: (1) the sense of it, (2) the mood
of it, (3) the attitude of it, and (4) the style of it. Keep these elements
in mind as you read, make notes or page references to indicate places
where each is effectively revealed, and include these in your report
when you write it.

REVIEW QUESTIONS

1. Why is your written paper the most important product your teacher
   has from which to judge you?
2. What are the three primary requirements for all written work?
3. What are the three basic obligations of all students toward written
   work?
4. What are some of the questions you can use to measure the quality of
   answers to written questions?
5. Of the ten rules for improving written work, which three do you consider to be the most important? Explain.

9

Acquiring Skill in Methods

Skill is the product of interest of the will and the commonsense application of a plan.

📖

Your coach gives you the rules, but only you can practice them enough to make the team.

INTEREST MEASUREMENT TEST

1. Do you think you could excel in any sport without practice?
2. Do you know certain traits of your own mind that lend themselves to some methods of study more effectively than to others?
3. Are you convinced that you can improve in all areas of mental skills?
4. Do you know what part of your waking hours are most productive for study?
5. Do you respect your own ability to accomplish whatever you set out to achieve?

PRACTICAL APPLICATION AND THE INDIVIDUAL

No methods of study will have value unless they are practiced until they become habits—as natural to you as the daily habits of dressing, eating, etc. We are born with traits that might point toward skill in tennis, football, or music, but without practice skill will not develop. This, too, is fundamental to good study habits—practice, and practice with a conscious awareness aimed toward improvement.

The law of habit without thinking is animallike. Yet many students drag from assignment to assignment without any self-assurance as to whether or not they are doing what is expected. To acquire skill in study you must discover and define the problem before you. All thinking originates in a problem, a doubt, a perplexity, or a difficulty. We are content to move by habit without thinking; we think only when we have to think. The student of poor habit, the student who starts without checking, does not see the problem before he starts his assignment, and when he finally stumbles upon it, does not know what it consists of or what to do with it. The person who thinks sees the problem or purpose of the assignment and knows exactly and precisely how to attack it because he has *checked.* He does not go over and over an assignment without knowing where he is going, or where he has been when he gets there.

There are many general, commonsense practices that aid in acquiring skill in study. You can acquire skill in study by giving yourself a fair chance. You cannot expect to develop a new set of habits overnight; it usually is wise to start with one or two good habits to replace the old, and practice these until they become regular routine. By improving slowly and making sure that the old habits are being put away for all time, the chances of success are greater, and there is little possibility that you will find improvement of study habits so much like punishment that you will revolt against the practices that would result in success and achievement. "Nothing succeeds like success," and if you can once taste the success resulting from new and better habits, you will improve from that day on.

Skill in study can also be acquired by association. Has it occurred to you to get constructive criticism from your teacher? There are many areas, perhaps foreign to you, a teacher knows well from years of experience. The teacher, for example, knows whether the vocabulary is learned more easily if it is written, what steps should be written in solving the problem, the best order for learning the chart, what the Q (Question) of your assignment is. Don't be afraid to draw from others' experience. Association with other students can also be helpful. Find out from the others around you why their grades are always better than yours? Is their written work neat and orderly to a degree that makes yours seem sloppy and disorderly? Do they have a written outline of the assignment? They can perhaps give you some good hints and would probably be willing to help if you will take the trouble to ask.

You can acquire the same degree of skill in study that you exhibit and execute in your favorite sport or hobby. It is *you* who must develop the feeling, the thinking, the willing.

Methods of study will, of course, require modification and adjustment from one course to the next. For example, the methods used to learn mathematics will be somewhat different from those used in studying history, but the basic principles of study are adaptable to all courses.

The individuality of each person will also determine to a large degree how one or another of the methods can best be used. Regarding study methods, the mind performs four functions in varying degrees of proficiency. These functions are: (1) receiving—through your gift of perception, (2) classifying—by your gift of judgment (thought), (3) preserving—laying away through your gift of memory, and (4) recalling—bringing back for use the impressions you have stored away. Remembering these four functions of the mind, and making a frequent estimate of the effectiveness of each in your own study habits, will enable you to discover your capacities and limitations in each area. Knowing how your own mind works is essential to adopting study habits which will best serve you, and from this understanding comes the self-confidence needed to achieve excellence.

VARIATIONS ON BASIC METHODS

All methods of study stem from the three basic skills of learning: (1) finding what you want, (2) fixing it in your mind, and (3) applying it successfully. You will notice little difference in some of the methods which follow. Having studied them closely, it would be wise to try each before you adopt any one for all or some of your subjects. One method might prove excellent for algebra but poor for history. Fit the method to the subject and to your own natural inclinations. Three items will occur in all the methods here offered. They are: (1) read, (2) question, and (3) review. With slight modifications as to approach, you will note that these constitute the principal ingredients of all good study habits.

One method widely recommended is the 4s = m formula. Interpreted, the formula means Four Steps = Mastery. The four steps in mastering the assignment are: (1) the preliminary survey, (2) reading the assignment for ideas and converting each paragraph, section, definition, etc. into questions, (3) the quick review—rereading those paragraphs, rules, definitions which you do not recall at a quick glance, and (4) summarizing the material studied briefly and logically in your mind.

The preliminary survey will use less time than any of the other three steps; but done properly can prove of great value.

The second step toward mastery—reading the assignment for ideas and converting small units into questions—contains three very important words: (1) reading, (2) ideas, and (3) questions. Reading as applied here means concentrating, remembering, applying—the primary aims of all good readers. Of the three methods of reading—(1) skimming, (2) careful, and (3) intensive—the method here applied would be intensive reading—reading to be understood clearly and remembered for purposes of application.

Now to read for *ideas* requires the reader to see groups of words rather than single words. Very few ideas are expressed in single words. Reading for *ideas* leads naturally to the *questions,* as shown by the question that each idea above fosters. Ideas that accumulate in a paragraph, section, or definition immediately become questions for the reader who has trained himself in this very important study habit. For indeed it is the formation of the question that gives most help to the mind's functions of laying away for future use and recalling when application is desired. In most assignments, application is almost always answering *questions* in class—the questions you have formed while studying, if you have chosen wisely.

The *quick review,* step number three in the mastery of an assignment, is beneficial not only to check against incompleteness in preparation, but provides excellent training for increasing one's speed in reading, recall, and comprehension. The method of reading used for the quick review would be *skimming*—fast reading to check or find a particular thing. When the skimming reveals parts not recalled, the reader will then return to *intensive reading.* One aim of all good study habits is to work more effectively within a limited time. You should use the third step for assignment mastery as a training period for speed. In fact, to go back over material at a snail's pace is likely to lessen the power of concentration and produce confusion rather than clarification.

The fourth step in mastery of the assignment—*summarizing* the material briefly and logically—has sometimes been referred to as "wrapping up the package." In a sense this is an apt description, for by this step you prepare your goods for presentation when called upon to display them in the classroom. Summary writing and outlining are covered in detail in another part of this book. Both can be used effectively in mastering your work.

However, much can be gained by the practice of oral summarization—a mental blueprint. Form your mental picture upon these logical elements: (1) what the assignment encompasses—that is, its dimensions—beginning and end; (2) the steps or order by which it moves—how one topic or rule leads to the next; (3) the proper judgment in choosing important key ideas—ideas which will aid in recalling tangent ideas if they are needed; (4) what was this assignment designed to teach—can its message or meaning be put in a single statement?

"But," you say, "all these steps and questions will take so long. Besides, I always read my assignments three times. Sometimes I study one assignment two or three hours."

You can only be reminded that good methods of study are designed to shorten the time you need for study and have you accomplish more in the shortened time. You may also remind yourself that all reading is not study, and that sitting with a book in your hands is not necessarily reading. Sometimes it is dreaming.

Perhaps you would like to try another formula, basically not too different, but with slight variations. Dr. Francis P. Robinson suggests a brief survey to locate core ideas, then following the Q3R method of study.[1]

The Q represents question. After the brief survey has been made, there should come to mind the Master Question—What am I going to learn? However, many students fail to prepare their minds psychologically to learn by omitting this valuable yet simple beginning.

The Q3R formula puts the questions before the reading. The section and paragraph headings are suggested as possible starting points for the questions. Turn the headings into a question and then read to answer your question.

The 3R of the formula stands for *read, recite,* and *review.* After the questions have been formed on the paragraph, section, or block of material that can be handled, the reading is done for one thing only—to answer the questions. Having read to answer the questions, look away from the book and repeat the answers. This accomplishes the second R of the formula—*reciting.*

Preparation for *review,* the third R, can be made while reciting. A few key words can be put in outline form. When all sections are fin-

[1]Francis P. Robinson, *Effective Study,* Harper & Row, 1946, p. 28.

ished, the key words in outline or more detailed notes if preferred, provide the material for review. If questions and answers are easily recalled, the assignment is finished.

THE BEGINNING OF SUCCESS IS INTEREST

"What is learned should never be passively or mechanically received, as dead information which weighs down and dulls the mind. It must rather be actively transformed by understanding into the very life of the mind, and thus strengthen the latter, as wood thrown into fire and transformed into flame makes the fire stronger."[2]

It is the responsibility of the student to be interested. No one can be interested for you, and no one can increase your interest unless you so will. It is the basic obligation that you must take to class; it is the basic obligation which you must hold up to each assignment. In life it is the basic obligation you will carry into your life's work, or life will make you a person of no consequence or influence, going from job to job, thinking always that the grass will be greener on the other side of the fence, bored with things as they are because you were never interested enough to learn that it is only through ignorance that we are ever bored.

Being interested is the basic obligation that is necessary for success in whatever work you do. The artist is always interested because the artist is a performer who does whatever job he or she undertakes in the best possible manner and as nearly perfectly as possible. If you want to be educated you will have to be an artist in your pursuit of knowledge.

The experience of living does not always offer great variety or choice, and so it is with education. If you get an education you are going to study many subjects which you *think* you do not like, and truly you might *not* like them. T. S. Eliot says, "No one can become really educated without having pursued some study in which he took no interest—for it is a part of education to learn to interest ourselves in

---

[2]Jacques Maritain, *Education at the Crossroads,* Yale University Press, 1943, p. 50.

subjects for which we have no aptitude." If you learn enough about a particular thing or subject you will find that, much to your surprise, it is no longer boring.

Interest results from effort of the will—this is also sometimes given as the definition of concentration. The two are so closely connected as to prove fatal in some cases. The word concentration conjures up a picture of some little wheels that mesh and turn, or some intricate system of switches that must be set in the right order. If a student is not interested in a subject and refuses to expend the energy necessary to focus one's strength and will upon it, cries of anguish issue from the wheels not meshing or the power not being switched on in proper sequence. The teacher hears, "I just don't seem to be able to concentrate." And the same student on the same day will expose great power of concentration on the playing field or working at a hobby. Use the word concentration with care because it is too closely connected with interest to be used by students and parents alike as the overall excuse for lack of achievement. "It is," says Gilbert Highet, "an intellectual process. It is choice."[3] If you cultivate interest, concentration will become a great focusing force to draw you to the very heart and center of your work. Concentration does not and cannot exist where there is insufficient interest.

Interest in a subject is not inherited or produced by a magic word or sounding promise; it is acquired. First, you must find out why you are not interested—and in this you will probably need help. That a subject is difficult and requires too much work is not reason for lack of interest. If you cannot establish a reason for not being interested in a subject, a little conscientious study might change your attitude, for one day's success will go much further than a month's failure in stimulating interest.

Do not expect that all assignments or even all subjects will hold a natural interest for you. Mathematics may seem unrewarding or En-

[3]Gilbert Highet, *The Art of Teaching*, Alfred A. Knopf, Inc., 1950, p. 68.

glish boring, while history is much more meaningful to you. If mathematics is the subject you like least, have the courage to do that assignment first. Mastering a subject which does not appeal to you will give you confidence in your ability to do difficult things as you go through life. Life is full of little duties that carry no immediate appeal, but the individual who can tackle a job whether liked it or not is the one who is going to be successful and happy.

The effort of the will cannot be reduced to a simple formula or practice; interest cannot be learned as one learns a vocabulary or a law of science. Interest can be acquired best perhaps by starting with a determination that *there is scarcely any limit to what a human being can do if he is sufficiently interested.*

REVIEW QUESTIONS

1. Explain the four primary functions performed by the mind.
2. What are the three basic ingredients of all study methods?
3. Explain the 4s = m formula for study.
4. Explain the Q3R formula for study.
5. Amplify in a concise paragraph the statement: "The beginning of success is interest."

10

How to Study Languages

*Before the study of a peoples' language, survey their way of life.
It is a part of education to learn to interest ourselves in subjects for which we have no aptitude.* —T.S. ELIOT

INTEREST MEASUREMENT TEST

1. Do you know the vowel sounds in English?
2. Have you been taught the fundamentals of English grammar?
3. Do you see English words clearly when you look at them?
4. Do you pronounce your words distinctly?
5. Are you interested in arranging words in a sentence to produce rhythm and emphasis?

THE NATIVE PREJUDICES

The languages here referred to are those other than the one you grew up with, being for most of us English. The word "foreign" carries a remote and alien connotation which can scarcely be called real in the world in which we live—since we are only a few hours distant from people speaking Spanish, French, German, and Italian. And there was never very much that was foreign and remote about the classical languages, Latin and Greek. Every day we rely on them for words and phrases to supply us with terms for naming many of the things we use and root words which make the very foundation of our own language. So if you can avoid the use of the word "foreign" you will probably be taking the first step toward getting rid of a prejudice against studying languages other than your own.

Further aid in getting rid of a prevalent prejudice against other languages is to change your point of view. It is not entirely correct, as you sometimes feel, that you are forced to study language for the accumulation of credits. Successful study of language can be of great economic value. Imagine yourself in a position to be sent by your company or employer to a project or plant in another country. It happens all the time, and the lucky people to get the opportunity are those who have the language qualifications.

Another point of view you can adopt to help make language study more meaningful is its cultural value. It has already been noted in an earlier chapter that speech, man's greatest invention, is the thing that makes us what we call "human" rather than "animal," providing a memory for mankind—the basis of all culture and civilization. This heritage is just as significant in Hebrew, Greek, Latin, French, German, Italian, and Spanish as it is in English. You can, therefore, approach the study of language from the point of view that it makes possible one of the most broadening and cultural elements of your education.

Change in point of view is a first step in conditioning the mind for another and more essential change, if language is to be studied with any degree of success. The mind must rid itself of the aptitude crutch. The aptitudes of each individual are different in different subjects, but in no subject, except perhaps mathematics, is "lack of aptitude" used so frequently as an excuse as it is in language study. The student who does not understand the grammatical structure blames it on aptitude, when in reality he does not know equivalent grammatical construction in English—nor even the meaning of basic grammatical terms. The student who says he can't learn to pronounce French is the same person who does not hear his history teacher describe the evolution of the "law of nations" as a part of Roman Law, and misses it on the test. The weakness is not being able to learn to pronounce French and not hearing important items spoken in English is one weakness—poor listening ability. Lack of aptitude is a symptom, not a disease. The real trouble has its basis in poor work habits, in ineffective techniques, and lack of background information. Use effective study methods and do not worry about lack of aptitude, because if aptitude develops from anything it must be proper methods of work which result in change. "Learning," writes Dr. Theodore Huebener, "is essentially the process of change induced in a living organism by experience. . . . The final stage of learning is habit; the result of habit is still. Learning, then, is basically habit formation. To learn a new language means simply to acquire another set of speech habits."[1]

LEARNING A NEW LANGUAGE THE WAY YOU LEARNED ENGLISH

The new set of speech habits comprising a new language will be learned to a very large degree the way you learned the language you use daily. You learned English by starting with a few words, actually with a few sounds. You did not forget them after you had used them one day, as if they were part of an assigned vocabulary for Thursday. You used these sounds over and over again—practice and more practice. In time, you could think in terms of the words you knew without saying them aloud. Your parents were happy because they didn't have to listen to you practice saying the word "dog" dozens of times each day. This, of course, seems very juvenile, but if you learn a new language, "a new set of speech rules," practice, practice, and more practice is going to be a very important part of the program.

You will learn the order in which these new words are arranged to make sense from the rules of grammar and the structure of the

[1]Theodore Huebener, *How to Teach Foreign Languages Effectively,* New York University Press, 1959, p. 4.

language. You may learn to read some of the language, and to speak it, before you learn the technical elements of construction. You certainly did this with your English. But an important factor in studying a language is to reconcile yourself to the importance of knowing the fundamentals of grammar. Perhaps a good way to start would be with an honest admission that, having missed learning many of the grammatical terms in studying English, a little study of English grammar would save you from immediate deficiencies.

A second immediate necessity in the study of a language is keeping up with each assignment. In no subject is the importance of rigid adherence to a schedule of day-to-day preparation as important. Granted, it is neither advisable nor wise to get behind in a day's work in any class, but falling behind in vocabulary, reading assignments, idioms, and grammatical study in language is fatal.

THE STEPS OF PROGRESSION

Learning a language is to progress from one step to the next, and each requires mastery of the one preceding it. The steps are four in number. (1) You must learn the meaning of words before you can use them. (2) You must learn something about word order and idiom before you can use them to express an idea. (3) You must learn the various forms a word can take before you can use it in the right person, case, number, etc. (4) You must learn to pronounce the word in order to express what you have learned in the preceding steps.

There is a fifth step which few secondary school language students attain but it should be your aim, for to accomplish it is to save half the time spent in reading and writing language. To think in the language means that when you see the Latin, French, or Spanish word for dog, you do not translate it into English, but use it as you find it— *canis* (Latin), *chien* (French), and *perro* (Spanish). Accomplishing this, you are prepared to use another language the way you use English. You do not turn English words into other words before you use them—doubling the time necessary to produce a thought picture.

Practice learning to think in the language you are studying. Start simply; first pick out familiar objects and try to name them in the language directly, without first thinking of the English name; next, advance to simple thoughts about the object—the dog ran, the dog is gentle. This practice can lead to more complex thinking and mastery.

THE FOUR PARTS OF LANGUAGE LEARNING

The four parts comprising the total study of a language are: listening, speaking, reading, and writing. The suggestions in each area listed below will help you accomplish more, with a greater degree of achievement and understanding.

Listening

1. Start by learning what to listen for. The introductory chapter of your Latin book probably explains how easy Latin pronunciation is. Sounds in French, Spanish, German, etc. are also presented at the beginning of the study. This is the first step. The basis of all language is sound. It is important for you to remember this. Convince yourself that understanding from listening is the first experience in learning a language.

2. Listen with a dual purpose—for sound and meaning. Only when sound has meaning is it of use in understanding what is being said.

3. Listen with the aim of reproducing correctly the new and alien sounds of a new language. This is your way of acquiring the ability to pronounce the language.

4. Use all the listening aids available to you—language records, listening tapes, classroom drills, language courses offered on TV, people proficient in the language. As a child you learned English by listening, listening, and more listening, and then you were ready to speak.

Speaking

1. Do not try to substitute speed for accuracy in your practice. Many Americans slur over words and syllables, but inaccuracy in pronunci-

ation is not the way to master any language. It is well to remember, also, that oral fluency is one of the major emphases in most language courses today.

2. Practice in speaking the language you are studying should be constant. It is a skill that has to be developed just as skill at tennis, billiards, or dancing. Practice in speaking contributes to two additional skills necessary to language study—skill in reading and translating, and skill in understanding what is heard (thinking orally in the language).

Reading

1. The first aid to reading the language assignment is usually some kind of help that accompanies the reading material, such as notes covering special uses of particular words, idioms, unusual word order, etc. Always study the helps or *notes* which accompany the test.

2. Try to read the material first in the language without translating. This is contrary to the practice of most students, and you will perhaps say, "But I'm only reading because I have to translate." Very good, but if you do a first reading without trying to translate, the second reading and translation will be much easier, and take much less time. This is also practice directed toward the ultimate in language mastery—to read it as Latin or French without having to change it into English.

3. Learn to read the language by phrases (groups of words). Reading word-by-word is as fatal to understanding as the word-by-word practice is in English. The beginner will perhaps read a single word at a glance, but training away from this is imperative to both idiom and word order.

4. Read by giving the whole sentence a quick survey. For languages with word orders, such as Latin and German, this gives the words their relationship to each other. This is also an aid in giving the proper meaning to words that take different forms.

5. Always read aloud when possible. This gives reading the added function of improving your skill in pronunciation. It is also an excellent

way to do a little effective self-evaluation. You can cover your weakness by the gesture of silent reading, but reading aloud will quickly show where your weaknesses lie. Your basic reading habits in English, for good or bad, will to a very great degree be carried over into your language reading.

Writing

1. The vocabulary helps in a given lesson usually apply to the written exercises of the same lesson. Study all textbook material carefully before starting to write the exercises.

2. Writing is the best means of fixing attention on spelling, form, irregularities, and word order in the language. Correct written exercises are impossible without a background knowledge of the parts of speech and syntax.

3. The rules of neatness and order are equally as important to the ten Latin or German sentences, or the third declension, as they are to your other written papers. Leave one or two lines between sentences for writing in corrections. Number sentences for easy correcting, and be sure your paper is worthy of being displayed as a model.

AIDS TO VOCABULARY STUDY

The skills of listening, speaking, reading, and writing have no value without subject matter to be performed upon, and the subject matter of language consists primarily of a body of words and the rules that govern their use. Without a well-stocked vocabulary, performance is hopeless. Below are offered suggestions for helping build a better working vocabulary.

1. Master the vocabulary that accompanies each lesson. Make your own vocabulary cards, writing the word to be learned on one side and the English meaning on the other. If you are lucky enough to be studying two languages, write the meaning in the second language on the back also. Use 2 x 2 or some small size. Review your whole card file daily

until you know each word from the preceding lessons. When you are sure you know a word, remove the card and place it in an inactive file.

Printed sets of 1000 Vis-ed cards may be purchased, and are better than having no card system. However, there are distinct advantages to preparing your own. Culling the specific words of the day's vocabulary from the set of 1000 is quite time-consuming.

2. Vocabulary interest and aid can result from learning the names of everyday things around you. This is the way you learned your English vocabulary—naming the things familiar to you. Try this for your language. Set yourself a moderate daily attainment—five words. Select them from food, furniture, travel, study, amusements, etc., one from a separate area of your everyday life.

3. Learn each new word by four distinct steps. (1) Pronounce the word and spell it. (2) Study its meaning and any inferred meaning. (3) Use the word orally in a brief original sentence different from any example offered in your book. (4) Write the word and its meaning three times; if an idiom, write it five times.

4. Make a knowledge of cognates a major part of vocabulary improvement. Cognates are words which have grown from the same root and are usually similar in meaning, although often modified, and in some cases, changed completely. But it is easy to see that recognition of the common heritage would immediately put you on speaking terms with the strange word.

5. It would be difficult to find any area of study in which habit is more profitable or more useful than in vocabulary study. No one has ever learned vocabulary by passively staring at a list of words. You may be the unusual "sport" or exception, but if you risk it for two weeks and it doesn't work, you are in serious trouble for the rest of the year. Form your vocabulary habits wisely—give number three of these suggestions a trial of two weeks. It may prove one of your most effective study habits.

REVIEW QUESTIONS

1. Explain why no language, either ancient or modern, is really foreign.
2. What is often referred to as lack of aptitude for language is usually lack of foundation in what?
3. Explain the statement: "The final stage of learning is habit."
4. What are the four progression steps in learning a language?
5. What are the four effective steps in learning new words?

11

Letting Mathematics Serve You

*Mathematics is a way of doing things—Counting the legs
of sheep grazing in a field and dividing by four to get the number of sheep in the flock—Dividing by two if there is a field of
ostriches.*

📖

*Mathematics is the classification and study of all possible
patterns.* —W.W. SAWYER

INTEREST MEASUREMENT TEST

1. Write out the reasons why you like, or dislike, the study of mathematics.
2. Do you consider yourself to be a person who prefers the exact rather than the general?
3. Do you think a history of the development of mathematics would be interesting reading?
4. Would you agree that there is much of the poet in all great mathematicians?
5. Is your sole aim in studying mathematics to pass, or do you also look upon it as one of the best learning processes for teaching you to think?

THE NATURE OF MATHEMATICS

Why is mathematics the subject most enjoyed by one student and the most misunderstood (and indeed hated) by another? One has retained one's original excitement and interest that accompanies all new discoveries and learning, and has kept step and developed a competence that has produced a degree of success. The other somehow lost the original curiosity when the newness wore off; prejudices began to creep in, they stayed until they had become convincing and permanent; and all approaches to mathematics became impassable paths into the unknown. Thus a subject which could contribute greatly to the development of a person's ability to think becomes difficult and burdensome, usually bordering on failure.

But mathematics can serve you, can serve you profitably and with much pleasure, rather than your serving it as a resentful slave, waiting to finish the last required course so you will be free forever. And in this last thought you are sorely mistaken. You will not be free unless you have an appreciation of the concepts of mathematics. You will not lose your interest in the world around you and the universe beyond you; and freedom to enjoy much of both depends upon a basic knowledge of mathematics, and how it has been used by others to unveil the secrets of earth and sky.

Where can we start to make the study of mathematics not unlike the study of your other subjects? Perhaps the basic step, as with all subjects, is to develop an interest in the intrinsic value of mathematics in your own experience, and its importance to our whole education, society, and indeed our very existence.

To appreciate the value of mathematics it is best to approach it as a way of looking at things. The poet sees the world in one light, the mathematician in another, but there is more than a modicum of truth in the statement that "No mathematician can be a complete mathematician unless also something of a poet." It therefore follows that if you enjoy looking at things in your literature class, through the eyes of the poet, you are capable of enjoyment by looking at things as seen through the eyes of the mathematician.

It is unreasonable to let prejudices or immediate difficulties hamper the cultivation of a mathematical outlook. Living in an age when the universe and space are the concern of everyone, one can no longer even remain unaware of the great part of our very existence that passes unexplained unless there is some knowledge of mathematics. Surely, none of us would choose to live in a less interesting world. Only on the surface of our own little planet Earth can we actually measure length, breadth, and distance, laboriously and at a snail's pace—foot by foot, yard by yard, and mile by mile. But when we want to measure the heavens, the path of a space rocket, when it will be over the Potomac River or Sydney, Australia, we send the fleet-winged courier, mathematics, to measure the far-flung corners of the earth and sky. So mathematics has value in giving us knowledge about a great many things around us on earth, and is almost totally responsible for what we have learned, and can yet learn, of the solar systems and universe where we cannot go out with yardstick in hand, but must travel, even in a space age, on mathematical wings.

THE BENEFITS DERIVED FROM MATHEMATICS

The practical aspects of a mathematical outlook are too obvious and numerous to detain us here. From checking the numerical grade on a paper, determining the returns of your investment at five percent, to estimating how many miles your car goes on a gallon of gas, or whether or not sheep can be profitably raised in New England—for all these, and a score of other problems to be formulated and solved daily, we turn to mathematics.

In addition to making the world around you more interesting, and providing an indispensable part of your operative daily existence, mathematics as a specific school subject can serve you in the following ways.

1. It can improve your ability to think clearly and with precision. For although there is a great deal of memorize-recall-apply procedure in the study of mathematics, it lends itself to a refreshing amount of creative thinking—applying old patterns to new things, often using "the hunch or guess" (the most creative thinking of all) to find a new principle or relationship that was not anticipated in the question presented by the problem.

2. One of the most significant and practical benefits that can come from the study of mathematics is the improvement of one's powers of observation. No reading requires keener observation of what exactly is written and precisely what is being asked. Powers of observation sufficient to visualize a condition or pattern are also necessary for the solving of problems. A man whose lot was 150 feet wide, wishing to build a fence across it with a post every 10 feet, went to the hardware store and bought 15 posts. In school he had apparently not let his mathematics courses serve to improve his powers of observation. When he had installed his 15 posts, he had to make another trip to the store.

3. The study of mathematics, accompanied by its history, can provide confidence in, and respect and appreciation for the marvelous workings of the mind of man. Perhaps the most important single means of clearing away some of the stumbling blocks of attitude would be to go back and search out the fascinating history of how men invented numbers to count by, first on fingers, thus our decimal system of ten, then using many more by doubling tens. We could learn how the Babylonians kept their records. Or how Eratosthenes, with a deep well in Syene, Upper Egypt, and a posthole at Alexandria, a distance of 574 miles and an angle of 7° 12, calculated the circumference of the earth to be 24,662 miles—missing by only 195 miles or less than 1 percent. Or we could study Euclid, whose geometry takes second place only to the Bible in terms of the period of time it has remained in use, or Pythagoras and his theory, which the Babylonians probably knew long before him, or Archimedes, perhaps one of the half-dozen greatest

mathematic brains who ever lived. We read the lives of poets and statesmen to appreciate their works. The same can be done with much pleasure in the march of mathematics and the men who have made it.

PREREQUISITES FOR EFFECTIVE MATHEMATICAL STUDY

Accepting the mathematical outlook and the specific benefits as desirable, the next step toward making mathematics serve as an effective learning process is to determine whether or not most inadequacies in dealing with numbers do not go back to deficiencies in the elementary skills of addition, subtraction, multiplication, and division. The student who has difficulty with elementary skills is usually also the victim of a larger than average number of careless mistakes. But are these not the same problems that occur in other subjects. If the basics of good sentence structure were missed, fragmentary and awkward sentences will often mar your papers. If you misspell certain words week after week, is this not carelessness? So why is there the built-in feeling that mistakes and shortcomings which occur when dealing with numbers are inevitable—somehow decreed by the gods before you were born to plague you the rest of your life?

There are available tests in the basic skills, the handling of fractions, use of equations, and solving simple word problems, that can be used to indicate areas where mistakes occur most frequently. Such a test is the sample Scholastic Aptitude Test which can be had at your school. Your teacher would be glad to prepare a test for you. Perhaps weaknesses could be determined by a tabulation of types of mistakes made on homework papers. Once the trouble areas have been discovered, the same sensible steps of checking, awareness, and neatness that are applied to produce satisfactory results in other subjects will reap a similar harvest in mathematics.

Proper outlook, positive thinking, and correcting obvious weaknesses bring you to the starting point for a pleasant and profitable mathematical experience. The suggestions that follow provide the tools to make this a fruitful learning experience.

HOW TO MAKE MATHEMATICS SERVE YOU

1. Apply the principle of *total* participation to everything that takes place in the mathematics classroom. Listen to the teacher's explanations and ask for clarification whenever a doubt arises. Copy sample problems and save them for homework help and examination review. As the teacher teaches, try to determine the pattern or theory behind the problem being discussed, and how it might be applied to other problems.

2. Make the vocabulary of mathematics the first element of study in all mathematical subjects. Although the scope of mathematics has increased more in the past three generations than it did in the twenty-two centuries from Euclid to Einstein, the vocabulary of mathematics has grown even faster. As a matter of fact, mathematics has almost a dual vocabulary—the old and the new. The so-called "New Mathematics" gives new and broader meaning to old patterns and concepts through a *new* vocabulary. The old words—addition and multiplication—are still in use, but new words—arrays, sets, group, field, and a whole covey of words ending in *morphism* (meaning form) are now found in your math book. You will need to use the definition of the particular book you are studying, so the index should be used as a guide to review basic words until you know them. Reference has been made to the importance of a basic vocabulary list for each subject, arranged in a notebook for handy use. For a mathematics course the symbols of manipulation are a very essential part of the vocabulary and must be included along with a brief definition of each.

Such a mathematics vocabulary is indispensable; it should begin, of course, with a definition of the word *mathematics,* which you have been using for a long time. But have you bothered to find a good working definition? W. W. Sawyer in his book, *Prelude to Mathematics,* gives this one: "Mathematics is the classification of all possible problems, and the means appropriate to their solution."[1] He rejects this definition as too broad, and offers another: "Mathematics is the classification and study of all possible patterns." He defines *pattern* as "any kind of regularity that can be recognized by the mind." Continuing, he adds, "Life, and certainly intellectual life, is only possible because there are certain regularities in the world." Not until we understand his vocabulary—pattern, regularity—do we understand his definition. The little symbols we call numbers, a legacy from Hindu writing and Arabic numbers, have no meaning except as they are directed by vocabulary. How would you define arithmetic after all these years of using it? One dictionary says it "is the science or art of computing by positive, real numbers." Perhaps you would prefer Carl Sandburg's definition: "Arithmetic is where the answer is right and everything is nice and you can look out of the window and see the blue sky—or the answer is wrong and you have to start all over and try again and see how it comes out this time."[2]

3. Make order, precision, and thoroughness the conscious implements for studying the textbook, doing the homework paper, and writing the test or examination. Order begins with studying the arrangement of the subject material of the textbook; it includes the arrangement of examples and problems on your homework paper, the neatness of the paper, and is evident in the format, distinctness with which the last number, sign, and decimal is written on your test and examination papers.

Precision means that the text assignment is studied so that each rule, theory, pattern, and principle can be applied. All examples, illustrative materials, and process rules are studied before written work is begun. Word problems are approached: (1) to visualize the problem, (2) to find out what is given, (3) to determine if what is given is clear, (4) to decide what is needed (asked for), and (5) what process or combination of processes are to be used in finding what is asked for.

Thoroughness is the means whereby you make sure. It involves putting all the steps of the problem on your paper. It includes check-

[1]W. W. Sawyer, *Prelude to Mathematics,* Penquin Books, 1955.
[2]Copyright, 1950, by Carl Sandburg. Reprinted from his volume *Complete Poems* by permission of Harcourt, Brace & World, Inc.

ing each step for errors, and then checking the completed product. It requires that the specific answer be checked if the problem is such that it can be.

These are the things, available within you, that can make mathematics serve you with new thoughts and a new "way of looking at things." Legend has it that over the doorway of Plato's Academy was inscribed "Let No Man Ignorant of Mathematics Enter Here." It is within your power to know that, had you been there, your entrance would not have been denied.

REVIEW QUESTIONS

1. As a specific school subject what are the three general areas of im-provement which mathematics provides you?
2. Proper outlook, positive thinking, and the correction of obvious weaknesses are necessary prerequisites for what?
3. What is meant by the "principle of total participation" in the mathematics classroom?
4. What are the three "conscious implements" necessary for the effective study of all phases of mathematics?
5. What are the five steps in the "precision approach" to word problems?

12

How To Study Science

*Give me a place to stand and a lever and a fulcrum and I can
lift the world.* —ARCHIMEDES

*Give me the right word and the right accent and I will move
the world.* —JOSEPH CONRAD

*The scientist never takes two steps at a time, and neither can
you.* —LOREN EISELEY

INTEREST MEASUREMENT TEST

1. Do you feel that science deals with facts while religion deals with values, and that consequently there can be no conflict between the two?
2. What do you consider man's greatest invention?
3. What do you consider man's greatest discovery?
4. Do you agree that "necessity is the mother of invention"?
5. Have you read a biography of Louis Pasteur, the person without whom six members from your class of twenty-four would not have lived beyond the age of five?

THE CHARACTER OF THE SCIENTIST

. . . The scientist is possessed by the sense of universal causation.

The future, to him, is every whit as necessary and determined as the past. There is nothing divine about morality, it is a purely human affair. His religious feeling takes the form of a rapturous amazement at the harmony of natural law, which reveals an intelligence of such superiority that, compared with it, all the systematic thinking and acting of human beings is an utterly insignificant reflection. This feeling is the guiding principle of his life and work, in so far as he succeeds in keeping himself from the shackles of selfish desire. It is beyond question closely akin to that which has possessed the religious geniuses of all ages.[1]

The artist with brush, the poet with pen, the philosopher with meditations, and the scientist with experiments—all have one thing in common. Each is trying to make, in a manner pleasing to him, an intelligible picture of the world, and to use the world each constructs as a means of escaping the narrow dreariness that so often encompasses everyday experiences.

YOU AND YOUR SCIENCE ASSIGNMENT

Your own science course in school, whether general science or biology, chemistry, physics, etc., can deepen your appreciation of the world in which you live, and add new dimensions of that world. The study of science will demand an exactness in reasoning, a precision in observation, and a thoroughness in execution, similar to that required of you in mathematics, for of course mathematics is the beginning of science.

The study methods applied to a general textbook reading assignment will also apply to science: (1) the preliminary survey with its accompanying question—What am I supposed to learn from this assignment? (2) the selective reading—intensive for all rules, theories, and formulas—careful reading for illustrative material; the reading to

[1]Albert Einstein, *The World as I See It*, Philosophical Library, 1949. Quoted by permission of the Albert Einstein Estate.

be accompanied by a thorough study of all graphic material (diagrams, charts, etc.); (3) reciting the material to yourself by scanning topics and signals such as boldface type, italics, and enumerations; (4) reviewing those sections that do not come immediately to mind.

The principles of order, precision, and thoroughness required in the execution of the written work of mathematics should be applied with equal care to science papers. For some written work in sciences like biology, a little painstaking artistic work (contrasting colors, etc.) can add much to show your teacher that you have that indispensable element for excellence—a sense of pride in your work.

SCIENCE AND FUNDAMENTAL WORDS

Fundamental to the study of science is the master list of several important parts of the particular course, be it general science, biology, chemistry, or physics. All students should keep, from the first day of the course, a master list of technical and specialized words and terms that constitute the scientific vocabulary of the course. Some of these words are new and difficult to spell. The application of language sense and relationship can help greatly in this respect, for many of them, or their roots, have been seen in Latin or French. Some science students find review easier if the master list is put on cards rather than in a science notebook.

The second master list should contain theories and laws that recur with such frequency as to be primary to understanding cumulative cases and problems. These should be stated as briefly as possible and the page number of the text where they are described in full should be written beside each.

The third master list should contain the distinctive formulas, equations, devices, and properties essential to working out the concepts or principles of the subject. This master list will be quite different in size from one science subject to another, and for the sake of workability should be kept to a minimum.

APPLYING THE KNOWN TO ARRIVE AT THE UNKNOWN

The master lists provide the basic working material of the science course. Having learned these, the mastery of the subject is largely dependent upon the student's capacity to solve word problems—applying what is known to arrive at the solution (the unknown). It is in a very real sense vocabulary ability—that is, deriving patterns and practical situations from numerical and linguistic forms of language that have been given. If you can think of your science course in this light, it will become much easier. Definitions, interpretation of formulas (and in these symbols take the place of words), and the handling of problems, are understood or misunderstood in proportion to vocabulary knowledge. Specific caution should be taken in reading formulas. They cannot be read as a word statement. The symbols have to be transposed to relay their meaning in words to the reader, and this requires very slow and careful study. Most difficulty with formulas arises from the student's expecting the symbols to give the message. Failing this, confusion results and the cry "hopeless," without ever carrying the work of understanding to its logical conclusion—transposing the symbolic picture into a real thought picture—made clear by words.

MODELS AND GRAPHIC LEARNING

There is much in the content of all science subjects that lends itself to demonstration by models. With a supply of wire and soft wood blocks, some cardboard and a box of colored pencils, you are provided with the material for the most effective of all learning processes—learning by doing.

In the realm of learning by doing, the diagram, the sketch, and the illustration, the graph, and the table, can also be of great value in understanding the text and operating with a degree of excellence in the laboratory. Since the study of science demands exactness, each of the figures named above is designed to perform a specific function.

A diagram shows relationships. It deals mainly with how one factor affects another as changes are introduced. Diagrams have their greatest use perhaps in showing cycles, such as the cycle of oxygen or carbon, or the action of sunlight on chlorophyll to form carbohydrates in living plants from water and carbon dioxide—photosynthesis. Diagrams may also be used in series very effectively to show phases or steps in logical sequence.

The sketch is designed to make clear by reasonable reproduction. It is a teaching and learning device that is older than speech. It is useful in cutting down the quantity of class notes, is excellent for showing how parts interact; and as an aid to learning, fulfills the old adage that "a picture is worth a thousand words." The sketch must, of course, reflect a background of study showing that you understand the nature of the object. To this should be added a sense of proportion, neatness, and your full ability as a painstaking and careful artist. The illustration evolves from the sketch, and presents as nearly a perfect reproduction as possible—the difference between sketch and illustration lies in the respective words used to define them—reasonable and perfect (perhaps faithful would be a more sensible word than perfect).

The graph, closely related to the diagram in form, performs the function of comparing two or more things by enumerative or graphic measurement, whereas the diagram shows interplay or effect of one factor upon another. The table, which is used in all science subjects, is a convenient and graphic way of making information visually understandable and also of showing relationships. In addition to the many tables found in your science textbooks, you can use tables to show progression of events, growth, items and functions, etc.

THE SCIENCE LABORATORY

In all science study, work done in the laboratory is essential to understanding and application. Laboratory activity centers upon learning by doing. It is designed to provide concrete observation, investigation, and discovery. The student who thinks in terms of a scientific career should use the laboratory for developing technical skills in dealing with equipment as well as learning the subject matter of the course through experimentation.

Observing certain laboratory rules of conduct and procedure can be most profitable. This particularly relates to conduct, since many students tend to make the laboratory a social meeting, a place to roam around disturbing others, experimenting wildly and carelessly, sometimes breaking valuable equipment. Use the following suggestions in your laboratory periods.

1. Laboratory study is designed to correlate experimentation and application with the material studied in the regular class and requires the same quality of attentiveness and concentration.

2. Avoid trying to do too many experiments. It is far better to bring one to a successful conclusion than have a number of indefinite measurements or applications.

3. Perform experiments only after sufficient study has been made so that the outcome of the experiment can be predicted.

4. Aim at the verification of what is already known, and move from the known to the unknown when directing an experiment toward discovery. Much material and energy is wasted by the student who ignores directions, operates after the manner of a boy with his first chemistry kit, and of course accomplishes nothing.

Reasoning in the science classroom and laboratory follows the five steps we use in all reasoning.

1. All thinking (reasoning) has its origin in a problem. The problem may be a situation, a perplexity, a question, or an actual mechanical, mathematical, or scientific problem.

2. The application of experiences or speculations as to the solving of the problem. Psychologists often refer to this step of reasoning as "sensory inference" and "implied solution suggestion."

3. Putting into effect the mind's choice of experience or speculation (theory, formula, etc.) for solving the problem. This is the process, moving the chair from one side of the room to the other until the right spot for it is found—doing the reasonable steps to arrive at the answer to the mathematics problem, or mixing the elements in chemistry to produce the compound desired.

4. The statement of final conclusion, solution, or summary; the nature of the statement dictated by the nature of the problem.

5. The test of the truth, correctness, or workability of the solution reached. Be sure to ask the question; given what I know about the problem, is my answer *reasonable?* Many a slipped decimal point has been discovered by asking this simple question.

Remember the five steps in reasoning and applying them to the study of science is in reality what "the scientific method" of procedure requires. Its five steps proceed from the following: (1) gathering data, (2) classifying and organizing data, (3) generalizing to get principles and theories, (4) verifying generalizations by experiments, and (5) subjecting results to verification and proof.

To all the good study methods, rules of neatness, exactness, and thoroughness, background knowledge can add incentive and interest to make the study of science more meaningful.

REVIEW QUESTIONS

1. What do the scientist, the poet, the philosopher, and the artist have in common?
2. What are the four steps for mastery of a science reading assignment?
3. Name and explain the importance of the three master word lists necessary for the effective study of science.
4. Explain the uses of the diagram, the sketch, the illustration, the model, the graph, and the table in studying science.
5. What are some of the things that you can observe personally to make the science laboratory a more effective place for learning.

Getting the Most Out of History

The interpretation that one makes of history determines to a large degree the direction of one's life. No one can escape history, and no one can avoid interpretation.

Not to know what has transacted in former times is to continue always a child. —LOREN EISELEY

The first chapter of history is exciting, the last chapter is sad.

INTEREST MEASUREMENT TEST

1. Have you ever tried to write your own definition of history?
2. Do you believe that history is the story of man's aim to attain the best for himself?
3. Is there a lesson in the philosopher's remark that unless we know the past we will be forced to relive it?
4. What would you list as the five most pleasant ways to learn history?
5. Do you believe that your life will be influenced by your interpretation of history?

HISTORY AND THE INDIVIDUAL

History is the story of mankind, and in its broadest sense, it is the story of everything that ever happened. History goes below the surface knowledge that each of us acquires by experience and gives life a third dimension.

Frequently the student who does poorly in history will try to defend lack of interest with some silly statement like "I am not interested in what is past, I am only interested in the present." If this sadly misdirected person could, by his own wishes, rid himself of history he would in the twinkling of an eye reduce himself to the basic survival instinct and intellectual level of the lower animals.

Let us, using a case that seems within the realm of possibility, rid our person who has no interest in history from all contact with the past. Scientists are able to produce a gas capable of producing mass amnesia over a whole battlefront or city. Suppose enough of such a gas could be let loose to drift over the whole earth, following the prevailing winds over land and sea. Over the whole earth, progressively as the wind moved, history would be erased. The memory of the past, the total past, would be gone in an instance. The whole of mankind would be plunged abruptly into savagery. A person reading a book would stare blankly. Our friend who had no interest in the past, half way home from school, would wander aimlessly, not remembering even home. One could meet others wandering with blank expressions, even one's own parents, and neither would recognize the other. The point of the story is plain; if the past has no meaning, the present has no meaning, and there is no future.

So for each of us history is concerned with human knowledge and human need; and from the time when our ancestors first began recording the stories of men and things, they seem to have been gifted with a quality of mystic wisdom whereby they preordained or predetermined the goodness and necessity of their story for all who would come after them. The unknown biographer who wrote the deathless life of David in the *Book of Samuel* did not know what he was stamping "the great man, the great person" as the miracle of history. Herodotus, as has been written of him, "probably never asked himself what history was good for," but he found it a good and wonderful quality of entertainment. Thucydides found in history a deeper and more useful good—lessons for the future from the incidents of the past. The patterns of the good of history have continued down through the centuries. Each generation rewrites the history of the world in the light of new problems facing it, and its concern is ever with the human knowledge and the human necessity of each individual who comprises its generation.

A SENSE OF PERSPECTIVE

Students frequently fail to get the most possible from history because they view it somewhat after the manner of the five blind men feeling the elephant. The results are an awareness of parts only—names, dates, events without relationships, and places without geographical or cultural implications; seeing, as it were, the trees without the forest. The true perspective of history is not the view through a microscope, and even a telescopic lens is not sufficient. One needs to look at history from a cycloramic point of view, supplemented by sufficient reflective power to mirror the observer himself. For only by seeing one's self as a part of the whole story of universal history can the meaning become clear and meaningful. It is commendable to know the date when Lincoln was born and the exact moment when his heart, sufficiently large to love all mankind, stopped on that fateful April morning in 1865. But it is far more important to understand, or at least ponder, why men of earth rise up and destroy the great among them. It is far more important for the history student to ask himself what part he or she has played in the assassinations before and after Lincoln. For if it is people who make people as they are—what have we made in our making?

After your parents, and perhaps one or two teachers, the greatest influence upon your life will probably be your interpretation of history—which is perspective, how you look at the world and events, and the judgments you make concerning the truth or falseness, the rational or the irrational, the good or the bad. If you delve deeply into the lives of the characters who have ennobled life and left the world better than they found it, you will probably generate within your own life a natural feeling for doing what is right. Finding the best in history, applying it to your life, reading your own life into the story that is history—this is the perspective you must achieve.

Only when you have learned to think historically can you put yourself into history. Everyday experiences teach us that to get the most out of something, we must take an active part and become completely involved, to the extent that we feel that we are a part and "belong." Belonging leads to a feeling of relationship. Relationship historically leads us to an appreciation of something bigger than ourselves. Almost every human being believes that there is a great intelligence, or cause, or guiding force, behind all our existence. Thinking historically helps us become more aware of a relationship that makes it possible for us to be more stable, more capable of accepting conditions beyond our immediate control, seem more worthwhile to the world around us, and find better reasons for our existence.

METHODS OF STUDY

The study methods for mastering a reading assignment apply, naturally, to your history assignment. If you use the PSQ3, method (preliminary survey, question, read, recite, review), as has been analyzed in detail earlier in this book, you are probably using the best method of attack. The history textbook lends itself to the preliminary survey better than perhaps any of your other books. When it comes to the Q—What am I supposed to learn from this assignment?—the question relates to more than a few facts to be mastered for recitation. The question in the history assignment implies the application of what is called "the historical method."

"The historical method" is the student's best training ground for becoming efficient in making sound judgments; for "the historical method" consists of those processes by which truth is separated from falsehood, fact is distinguished from opinion, effects are measured in the light of causes, and conditions and situations are weighed in relationship to probability and consequence.

The steps in execution of the 3R's (read, recite, and review) are the same as discussed in an earlier chapter. It should be noted in passing that the concentration required in using the "historical method" in the mastery of a history assignment demands a tremendous expenditure of energy. It is doubtful if many students can maintain the sustained concentration necessary to understanding for more than twenty or twenty-five minutes at a time. The student should judge when concentration falters and relax for a five-minute interval. The effortless gazing upon a page, or reading history as one reads a novel, is of no value and the total time consumed in such attempts to absorb by some magical transposition from printed page to mind is wasted.

Three classifications of words should always be utilized in mastering a history assignment: (1) the basic words of history that form the fundamental vocabulary and terminology of the course, (2) the key words which modify and qualify historical fact out of the realm of the general, and (3) signal words that introduce important elements of the assignment.

Basic vocabulary has been noted as necessary in all school subjects, but history seems to be the most neglected in this area. The difficulty seems to arise from the fact that many basic vocabulary words of history are heard so often in ordinary conversation that the student assumes that their meaning is commonly accepted. But history demands an exactness beyond the general idea that the student may have of the meaning of such words as: government, culture, civilization, revolution, democracy, republic, civil power, municipal, franchise, commonwealth, judicial, ideology, tyranny, bureaucracy, autonomy, mandate, alliance, treaty, nation, state, State, communal, etc. Write down one or two definitions from the list above. Check for accuracy by using your dictionary. Misunderstanding and misinterpretation result from basic vocabulary definition, and in history this failing can be fatal to both grade and one's own philosophy of life in community. Familiarity is not sufficient for the basic history vocabulary words; only the exact meaning will give full understanding to history.

Key words qualify and give specific definition to the meaning of history. They are important because they remove historical statement from the area of generalization into the realm of the definite. The *Near* East is something quite different from the East; *domestic* policy is not all policy; *geographical* influences mean something specific; *natural* boundaries refer to a specific kind of boundaries as distinguished from lines of demarcation or man-made boundaries. *Near, domestic, geographical, natural,* are key words. Learn to recognize and underline the words in your history book that narrow the meaning of a statement. This is a practice which will help you train yourself away from generalizations in speaking and on tests—a fault almost universal among history students.[1]

In studying your assignment certain words will almost say, "What follows is important; don't miss it." These are called *signal words.* They introduce parts of your assignment which are to be carefully noted. Some signal words are: examples, results, details, significance, principles, essentials, innovations, comparison, contrast, influences, causes, effects, facts, implications. Along with signal words go number signals. Many historians number important things or introduce them by a number signal word. For example: *Four* great *innovations* came about to change The Old Stone Age into The New Stone Age. They were: the making of tools by grinding, the domestication

[1]Adapted from William H. Armstrong, *You Can Boost Your Grades in Ancient History.*

of animals, the development of agriculture, and the making of pottery. The historian might have omitted the number (Four) signal (innovations) words, and written The Old Stone Age became The New Stone Age when: (1) men learned to make tools by grinding rather than chipping, (2) animals were domesticated, (3) agriculture was discovered and developed, and (4) men learned to make pottery. In either case you have been signaled "here is something important."

Your history notebook, if properly kept and arranged, can be a great factor in making review for tests and examinations much easier. A good history notebook should be divided and labeled. Your teacher will probably direct you, but here are some divisions which are a must:

1. Your *basic vocabulary* words with definitions of those you find difficult to remember.

2. All test questions. Examinations are usually made up of questions that have been given on tests.

3. Charts, outlines, maps used independently of the textbook, or copied from the blackboard.

4. Notes on material covered in class that are not in your textbook. For example: In your textbook you study the war between the Greeks and Persians. In class your teacher tells you about Herodotus and his history of the war. Just a short note in your notebook: "Herodotus, who is called the father of history because he was the first Greek to write history as an exciting story, wrote the history of the Persian wars." When test or examination comes, that little note might boost your mark in two ways. It would make your answer more complete than the textbook material, and recalling it might help you recall some details your teacher might have told you from Herodotus's history.

Use the *who, where, when,* and *why* method for remembering the details of your history lesson. Put the *person* in the *place* at the right *time* and know the reason *why.* The four *W*'s make a complete picture. They bring the parts of the puzzle together. For example: Leonidas, the heroic Spartan king (who) is at Thermopylae in northern Greece (where) in August, 480 B.C., (when) to guard a narrow pass (why) against Xerxes's invading army. The four *W*'s also make an outline upon which the whole exciting, heroic story of Leonidas comes back to you detail by detail. If you will practice the who, where, when, and why method for remembering your history lesson, you will find that many details, once lost, will remain with you. The four *W*'s method of creating a complete picture of events is used by newspaper writers to present a clear story, and by lawyers to present clear and complete evidence to juries in court. Use it for studying your history lesson.

The writer who wrote the history book you are studying did not mean that you should repeat (parrot-like) his very words when you are answering questions in class. Practice using your own words when you review your lesson. Even in your first reading of the assignment, if you find yourself with a group of words that do not seem to make a passage clear to you, put it in your own words.

This will not only help you remember your history, but will help you to express clearly what you wish to say. And the ability to put your thoughts into clear expression, to communicate your ideas to others, is the ability that, more than any other, will make you a success or a failure in life.

THINKING GRAPHICALLY AND PHYSICALLY IN HISTORY

The maps in your history book were put there for you to use. They show more clearly than any words can describe where you are going in your history. All graphic material, maps, diagrams, graphs, genealogy charts, simple designs, and illustrations are important visual aids to help you. Perhaps their value can be emphasized by pointing out to you that they cost more in time and money than any other part of your book. The writer of your textbook probably spent months or even years gathering the graphic material. The reproducing, printing, sizing, and placement in the text is expensive for the publisher. Remember, there is much truth in the old adage: "One picture is worth a thousand words." But don't forget to read the words under the picture; they were also put there to help you.

Diagrams may show what happens to surplus food produced by Babylonian farmers; they may show how the population of Egypt was arranged by social classes; they may show names and duties of the twelve chief deities of the Greek Pantheon (*pan*—union, *theos*—god; thus union or group of gods). Such diagrams may be animated to such a degree as to bring the information completely alive. They can be used to fix in your mind a permanent picture. For example. You read a description of Zeus as the King of the Gods, and of his associates and their special duties. A diagram showing Zeus on a throne wearing a crown; Ares, God of War, holding a sword; Hermes, with wings on his feet, fleet with his messages—and all are known at a glance.

Use diagrams to help you remember details; there is no better help. Practice making simple drawings of your own to visualize your lesson. After you have read how the stones were put into place on the Great Pyramid, draw a simple figure to illustrate the long earthen ramp up which the stones were moved. This is learning by doing, one of the best ways to learn.

MAKE GEOGRAPHY A THINKING PART OF YOUR HISTORY

Geography influences the whole life of a people. Geographical influences may range from the clearness of the skies over Greece to the number of goats roaming a mountainside. The sky with its incredible blueness reflected in the Mediterranean softened the harshness of the rugged mountain contours and gave the Greeks a perspective of beauty unequaled in the world. They set their white soft-lined temples against the blue skylines; a setting so natural that the temples seem to be a part of nature. Dreaming under their sunlit sky, they developed an art of living that is forever mirrored for the world in their cultural achievement.

Yet their daily existence was as severe as the hills and mountains around them. The goats that roamed the mountains ate the young tree sprouts. Forests to prevent erosion never had a chance to grow. The top soil washed into the sea, and the Greeks forever struggled to coax a precarious living from the land; so much so that a Spartan king once remarked: "Poverty is our companion from childhood." This same geographical influence sent the Greeks across the sea searching for better fields to cultivate; thus they spread their civilization over the whole Mediterranean.

Geography has always influenced history. Studying history make geography supply you with answers to questions that ask "Why?"

SUMMARY OF WAYS TO STUDY HISTORY

1. Set great value upon all history and your responsibility for knowing the past, "lest you be condemned to relive it."

2. Develop a cycloramic perspective of history that goes beyond names, dates, events, and includes the whole and its meaning, including especially the meaning as applied to your own experience.

3. Use the five-step method of study: (1) preliminary survey, (2) question—What am I supposed to learn?, (3) read, (4) recite, (5) review. Most history textbooks are properly designed for this efficient method of study.

4. Know what the "historical method" means, and use it in reading your history assignment.

5. Put great stress upon the importance of the three classes of words so helpful in studying history: (1) basic vocabulary, (2) key words, and (3) signal words. Know the aid rendered by each.

6. Keep your history notebook in such a manner as to make it the chief source of material for review. Use the four designated divisions, and add whatever else may seem helpful.

7. Use the *who, when, where, and why* (the four W's) method of remembering details in your history assignment.

8. Learn to put the historian's thoughts in your own words. Do not try to learn and repeat (parrot-like) the vocabulary of the author of your history book.

9. Use all graphic material—maps, diagrams, pictures and captions, charts—to illuminate the subject.

10. Learn to think physically in relationship to cause and effect in history. Geography, economic conditions, even the air men breathe (whether fresh or saturated with smog) influence history. Do not overlook the world in searching for a detail.

REVIEW QUESTIONS

1. Explain what is meant by historical perspective.
2. Explain the meaning of the "historical method."
3. What are the five steps in the mastery of a history assignment?
4. Name and explain the function of each of the three classifications of words so important to the study of history.
5. Name and explain the aids of four types of graphic material available to make history more meaningful to you.

14

Tests and Examinations

"Whatever is worth doing at all is worth doing well."
— LORD CHESTEFIELD

📖

Nothing in a teacher's life is more rewarding than to receive a
paper, be it a list of ten words or an examination, that reveals
the writer's concern for order, neatness and excellence.

INTEREST MEASUREMENT TEST

1. Do you keep a notebook aimed at making review for tests and examinations easier when they come?
2. Are you afraid of tests, or do you consider them a challenge?
3. How frequently do you misread questions and write wrong answers as a result?
4. Do you prefer objective or essay type tests?
5. What percentage of test and examination questions are you able to anticipate as you review?

ATTITUDE TOWARD TESTS

Dr. Francis P. Robinson in his book, *Effective Study*, poses this question: "Did you ever thank a teacher for giving an examination?" At first glance you are not likely to find much in your thinking that would help generate an affirmative answer. The teacher does spend much time making out questions you are expected to answer; and after you have taken the examination, many hours of the teacher's time go into carefully evaluating the worth of your paper. Mistakes are marked so that when your paper is returned you can go over them, possibly even write in corrections so the same mistakes will not reoccur.

Do you, like many of your associates, consider the test or examination as a personal battle which the teacher wages in an attempt to defeat you, or a contest in which one tries to outwit the other? If this is your attitude toward tests and examinations you probably do one of two things when the teacher returns your paper to you. One, you throw it away without even bothering to do more than glance through it to see where points were taken off; or two, without checking an incomplete answer against the facts as studied, you approach the teacher demanding to know why points were taken off. This itself is, of course, the most negative of approaches. The whole attitude is contained in the difference between two questions: "Why did you take off points on this question?" and "What should I have included that I did not?"

Another attitude toward tests and examinations to be avoided is that of trepidation and fear. Fear of taking tests and examinations results in tension and disturbed thinking that produces blind spots (not being able to remember answers that you knew ten minutes before the test) and careless mistakes. This is the attitude of people who are afraid to venture into new areas in life; these are the people who visualize the new method, the better tool, the stronger bridge, but hesitate until someone else realizes their dreams.

Fear prevents success on tests and examinations, because fear conditions the mind for failure. The student who is afraid starts in a state of confusion and disorder, thus throwing away the advantages one has accumulated by preparation. The student who approaches tests and examinations in an attitude of fear is almost always characterized by the following: (1) Marks are considerably lower than daily recitation marks, sometimes as much as twenty points. (2) He complains about the teacher—not sufficient explanation, not conducting detailed review, etc. (3) Invariably finding fault with the test material—it is too long, not the type of question expected and studied for; didn't understand the wording of questions, read the word muckrakers instead of mugwumps and missed the whole point. (4) A check of the nature of preparation reveals a frantic last-ditch stand, loss of sleep to the point of almost total exhaustion, and not infrequently, loss of important notes or review material just when they were needed most. (5) Fear compels this person to study for the test with someone, and invariably choosing a study companion who has the same attitude of fear and whose knowledge of the subject is only equal to, or perhaps less than, one's own.

If two or more of these characteristics are behavior patterns you find yourself practicing at test and examination time, you should educate yourself out of them as quickly as possible. For entertaining them is to subject yourself to the climate of tension and fear, conditioning yourself for defeat.

There is, after the two negative attitudes, a third—wholly positive. It is the attitude of challenge, self-confidence, and a feeling of self-sufficiency toward content, sometimes called content-reliability. The student who accepts a test as a challenge to show the teacher the extent of his knowledge of the subject and to improve his grade is stimulated, which in itself produces the added energy needed to think clearly and act with precision over a longer period of concentration than the daily drills require. The attitude of challenge reflects itself in enterprising rather than burdensome preparation, and self-confidence grows out of this adequate preparation. There is no room for tension and fear. Even questions that stump you are approached with a calculated response so that worthwhile answers, although perhaps only partially correct, can be worked out. This is the attitude that assures the student that the relationship between student and teacher, and question and answer, must always be one of cooperative production rather than competitive destruction.

One of the first steps toward adopting a positive attitude of challenge and self-confidence toward tests and examinations is to understand the real purposes why these tests are necessary and what is gained in giving them.

REASONS FOR TESTS AND EXAMINATIONS

The reasons for rests and examinations are several, and are beneficial to both student and teacher. From the student's point of view the first reason is motivation. Few of us are self-disciplined and sufficiently motivated to educate ourselves without direction and requirement. Being held responsible for periodic testing of accumulated knowledge is a strong motivating force.

A second reason for rests and examinations is that they afford the student an opportunity to show the extent of his learning that daily preparation cannot provide. The student is given a chance to demonstrate ability to organize and unify large volumes of material, tending away from the fragmentation implicit in day-to-day assignments.

A third value to the student is to give insight into what the teacher considers most important. If tests ask for the main topics and essential principles, the student is able to estimate with some degree of accuracy the nature of what will be required in future and larger examinations.

A fourth important reason is that the student can discover both shortcomings and the extent of progress. By a careful study of errors, the areas from which they chiefly come, whether their pattern reflects difficulty in reading questions, taking sufficient notes, missing important review hints in class—once identified, steps can be taken toward correcting weaknesses.

The fifth value of tests and examinations to the student is that they constitute one of the most important learning processes. Decisions have to be made regarding appropriation of time, interpretation of facts, discrimination between essential and supporting ideas, and reasonable distribution of each. Indeed, tests and examinations may rightfully be called mind-stretchers.

REVIEWING FOR TESTS AND EXAMINATIONS

The most successful review is the one which starts with the second assignment at the beginning of the term and is followed as a part of daily preparation throughout the whole course. The elements of such a review would include a well-kept notebook, a basic vocabulary for the course, important class notes, all weekly and monthly test questions, and a well-marked textbook, indicating the material designated important during the course. In addition to the physical elements, there should be an interwoven mental blueprint, uniting the parts of the subject into a whole rather than a succession of parts.

The primary demand made by an examination is that of recalling large amounts of information. The objective examination requires only recall; the essay examination demands recall plus organization and amplification. Since effective recall depends upon study distributed over a long period of time, even the immediate review before examination should be extended over hourly periods of study, reaching back ten days or two weeks before the examination. Review should never be started later than a week before the exam. Five one-hour review periods spread over five days before the testing day are far more profitable than ten hours of attempted study the day before the examination.

The ten-hour session, or even a five-hour ordeal, the day before the examination, or worse yet, the all-night period of mental exhaustion and confusion, can in no way be described as review. It is a short-sighted, superficial, and utterly profitless struggle to cram a great deal of information into one's mind. At most "cramming" affords a smattering of information for short time use only, because it slips away quickly, usually starting even before the examination can be finished. Its chief product is to overlay what has been learned during the term with confusion.

Pages can be written on the disastrous effects of cramming, and case histories of its ill results and failure would fill volumes. Does it not suffice to leave its senselessness to be recognized by whoever is endowed with an iota of common sense, and learn ways to really make a review less a period of self-torture and more a period of profitable study?

SUGGESTIONS FOR SUCCESSFUL REVIEW

1. Learn to select what is most important to learn. General principles, formulas and experimental conclusions, vocabularies and rules, historical sequences and literary types, theories and facts, are some of the important items in your various courses. In selecting, be sure to differentiate between opinion and fact. Give particular attention to material that is emphasized by boldface type, questions, or repeated in summary paragraphs.

2. Listen during the two weeks before examination with a precision and relentlessness that allows you to miss nothing said in class. Even though the teacher might be continuing with new material in order to cover the required subject matter, there are telltale signs to indicate that important items for review are being made available to you.

3. Review by using questions to predict questions. When you have found what you consider important, turn it into a question, or ask yourself how it could be made into a question. This requires discipline, for many students choose the easy method of forming only questions that they can answer. But the easy questions are never the only ones on examinations.

4. Review by reorganizing your course material. Where possible, reduce the subject matter to easily remembered divisions. In mathematics it may be: definitions, word problems, theorems, formulas, general concepts. In history it may be: biography, chronology, reform move-

ments (radical), reform movements (conservative), domestic wars, foreign wars, economic problems, civic problems, religious problems.

5. Review by changing your point of view. If you have dealt with a subject during the term from the point of view of memorization for a credit only, change your point of view to that of application for understanding. The first point of view is a deterrent to successful study, the second is one of study's greatest psychological aids. And unless your mind is prepared, there can be no profitable review.

6. Make question "terminology" and question "reading" a part of review. Certain words appear in question after question, but these key words often mean different things to your several teachers. You must know what the teacher expects when the question says; explain, evaluate, state, relate, illustrate, enumerate, describe, interpret, define, diagram, compare, contrast, etc. Practice reading chapter-end questions to get the exact meaning of what a question asks for. Note the characteristics of questions that pertain to different subjects. Some subjects lend themselves to specifics, while questions in others are very general. Question "knowledge" should be an important part of any review.

TAKING TESTS AND EXAMINATIONS

Tests and examinations are generally of two kinds: objective and subjective. Objectives tests are short-answer tests which require recognition of correct answers among incorrect ones, and true statements set beside false ones. Objective tests also assess ability to recall material needed for supplying details left out of statements. Objective questions are usually of the following kinds: (1) Recall (filling in blanks); Joseph Conrad was born in _____ and spent his early years _____. (2) Recognition (multiple choice); Ghandi learned of civil disobedience from (a) Emerson, (b) Gladstone, (c) Lincoln, (d) Marx, (e) Thoreau. *Ans.* (   ). Also under recognition come True and False questions: Mockingbirds belong to the mimic family. (T) Mockingbirds belong to the sparrow family. (F)

A third type of recognition question is the matching question. For example: Write the number of the phrase which fits the character in the space provided:

1.	Founder of Hebrew Nation	2	Lincoln
2.	The Great Emancipator	1	Moses
3.	Apostle of Peace	4	Gladstone
4.	Three times Prime Minister	5	Einstein
5.	Scientist and Philosopher	3	Woodrow Wilson

Here are some things that should be considered in approaching objective examinations.

1. Pay particular attention to mechanical instructions, that is, instructions that tell you *where* and *how to* answer questions. Wrong position may result in wrong answers; but even if it does not, answering in ways other than are required may cause the teacher difficulty in grading your paper. Some teachers take off points for not following instructions.

2. The questions are often many in number and sometimes all are not meant to be answered. Regardless, answer the questions that you know first, and come back to any you wish to spend more time on.

3. Read certain types of objective questions (particularly True–False) with an eye set to observe all qualifying words. These words—usually, always, most, never, some—give insight into when and under what conditions a statement is or is not correct. Of all places where modifiers are used, they play their most important role in True–False questions.

4. All objective questions require correct reading if you hope to write the correct answer. Don't let premeditated opinion cause you to read into the question a word that is not there. This results in wrong answers, and after the examination you are heard to say, "But I thought the question was . . . "

5. Do not change answers too quickly as you check your examination before turning it in. Your first answer is always the most reliable unless you are absolutely sure you have made a mistake. If there is any doubt, *leave the first answer.*

6. Because there is not much to write on objective examinations, do not think that neatness and order can be ignored. Words and numbers can be written sloppily or neatly. Neatness begins with the first blank you fill in and ends with the way you sign your name at the end of the examination.

The second kind of test, the subjective, is a type of test that demands more of you in both recalling and organizing subject matter. These are usually called "essay" and may be short-answer questions (a paragraph) or discussion (demanding a lengthy essay, showing the student's entire scope of knowledge on a particular part of the course). The word subjective implies that this kind of examination is more personal than the objective. It provides you with a greater opportunity to show the extent of your preparation. And, conversely, it provides the teacher with a chance to make more personal judgments in evaluating the paper. For this specific reason you should think in terms of what judgment you would make of the answers written if *you* were the teacher.

Essay examinations measure your ability to recall what you have learned, organize it intelligently, and express it clearly, with meaningful interpretation, selection, or application, depending upon what is asked for by the question. The first and most important fact to remember regarding essay examination questions is that there is no such thing as a *general answer.*

Successful execution of essay examinations can be carried out by practicing a few essential requirements:

1. Read through all the essay questions before you start to write. Essay questions demand a rather precise allotment of *time* for each question. On many discussion questions you can write much more than time allows. A sketchy outline (oral or written) is almost a necessity

in allotting time needed for each question. If key words pertaining to the answer come to mind at the first reading, they should be written in the margin as future aids to recall.

2. When you are ready to answer the first question, having written the time allotted to it in the margin of your paper, you should read the question to determine exactly what it asks you to do, and what instructions are included for doing it. If Alexander's spiritual legacy is asked for, it is a waste of time to go into detail about the physical legacy (army, devoted generals, etc.) he received from his father. In the essay question it is again (as in objective questions) the qualifying word that gives the explicit meaning to the question. Yet, and tragically, some students read words into questions which are not there. The student who reads *muckrakers* instead of *mugwumps* may write a beautiful answer, but he will get no credit; his answer is to a question that wasn't asked. The qualifying words of a question are really the built-in directions for answering it. A record covering five years' careless mistakes on tests and examinations made by students showed carelessness in reading the question to be responsible for 64 percent of all careless mistakes.

3. Read the question a second time to determine the steps you will take in writing a quality answer. Decide the amount of material needed to produce a complete answer, not brief to the exclusion of important details, and never wordy to the extent of rambling generalization and meaningless quantity. The mental or key-word outline, begun at the initial reading of the examination, is now completed. Arrangement, significance, and accuracy of topics and accompanying details are mentally blueprinted. An effective opening statement is visualized, if possible, restating part of the question. An answer is never started with a pronoun without an antecedent. Two such beginnings, fatal to a good mark, but often used are: "It is when" or "It is because." Always make the subject of the question the subject of your answer. As the second reading is being done, constant alertness against anything that will give your answer an element of vagueness is essential.

4. As the answer is being written, keep in mind the teacher's preference for style of presentation, use of illustration to show understanding, and points you have gathered from the teacher as to what is considered a model answer. If you have had complimentary notations on earlier test papers for the way you handled an answer, try to apply the same method to as many questions as possible. Ask yourself the question: "What is the teacher's aim in this particular question?" Make your paper easy to mark. Use signal words and numerals to introduce important facts and series. Number questions to the left of the margin, and skip one or two lines between answers. Keep before you an awareness that the neatly written paper generally has fewer mistakes and is certainly easier for the teacher to mark.

5. Concentrate on one question at a time and use an invisible system of numbering important points in your answer. Students often "overwrite" or "write away from" questions, because they jump ahead and are thinking of a question to come. The teacher has not asked questions which require repeating subject matter, so be careful to keep all answers within limits set by the questions. An excellent method for avoiding generalizations (which have no value) and "padding" (for which you can be marked off drastically by your teacher) is to mentally number important points as you write them down the page. Illustrations, specific elaboration, important facts, explanations where needed to clarify your understanding of a definition or event, are necessary parts of a good "essay answer." The practice of invisibly numbering important items as you write will show you the difference between what has value (and will add to your mark) and what is worthless.

6. Check over the completed examination paper before you turn it in and when it has been returned to you after being graded. In allotting examination time, ten minutes for each hour should be reserved for checking when the writing has been completed—for a one-hour test, ten minutes, for a two-hour test, twenty, etc. Check for mechanical errors and obvious factual mistakes, such as wrong words, incorrect

conclusions, transposed characters, etc. As with objective tests, do not change anything in an answer unless you are absolutely sure it is wrong. Rely on your first impression.

Much can be learned about writing better examinations and using better methods of study by going over the graded paper when it has been returned. By checking against your book you can see what you omitted that the teacher considered important, or how in writing you misinterpreted the qualifying word in a question. If such errors are carefully noted you will not repeat them on the next test.

SUMMARY OF RULES FOR REVIEWING AND TAKING TESTS AND EXAMINATIONS

1. Review by selecting the important subject matter and concentrating on it rather than the trivial and incidental.
2. Review by having your listening tuned for hints and helps given by the teacher just prior to the testing.
3. Review by using questions—ones you predict for the test—on what may be asked on specific subject matter.
4. Review by reorganizing the subject matter into logical divisions, keeping the sense of unity by an awareness of relationships between parts.
5. Review by changing your point of view. Deal with a subject by letting your imagination add interest.
6. Review by knowing what "question words" mean. Learn what your teacher expects when certain key words are used.
7. In the test and examination read all questions and instructions carefully and repeatedly until you understand exactly what is required for the answer and presentation of the answer.
8. Know the general implications of key and qualifying words in both objective and essay questions. Do not, under any circumstances, make an exception to what the qualifying word asks for.
9. In objective tests give the precise answer, and in essay tests make the answer complete; remember always that quantity without quality will not get much of a grade.

10. Observe all rules of neatness, mechanics, and clarity. The attractive paper that is easy to read gets the better grade.

11. Check your paper carefully before it is turned in. Unless you are absolutely sure you have made a mistake, do not change your answers. The first impression, as psychological tests have shown, is more reliable.

12. Improve all future test and examination grades by carefully going over all returned papers. Note the shortcomings so as to not repeat them on the next test.

REVIEW QUESTIONS

1. Explain the difference between reviewing and cramming.
2. What are some of the ways one may change viewpoint in reviewing?
3. What are the two ways of looking at tests and examinations?
4. Explain the five reasons why tests and examinations are given.
5. What are the two types of examinations? What are some of the demands and advantages of each?

Index

About the Author

BORN IN 1914 in Lexington, Virginia, William H. Armstrong is best known for his 1970 Newbery Award winner, *Sounder,* and its sequel, *Sour Land.* He is a man of many talents: sheepherder, writer, scholar, and craftsman. He likes to write with a pencil that allows him to "feel the words" in a room overlooking the Housatonic River Valley, from where he can see the mountains in the distance. When asked his advice for students who think they might like to write, Mr. Armstrong answers: "Number one: read, read, and keep on reading. Number two: listen to your teachers. Number three: be proud of your written work. Dot the i's and cross the t's. Neatness grows from dotted i's and crossed t's into beautiful pages." The recipient of the National School Bell Award for distinguished interpretation in the field of education, Mr. Armstrong lives in Kent, Connecticut, where for over fifty years he taught history at The Kent School.

Study is Hard Work

has been set in Minion, a contemporary digital type family inspired by classic old style typefaces of the late Renaissance. Created by Adobe designer Robert Slimbach and named after one of the type sizes used in the early days of typefounding, Minion means "a beloved sevant," reflecting the type's useful and unobtrusive qualities.